# THE PREMIER GUIDE TO
# Swansea Bay

*Written and edited by*
Trevor Barrett
*Managing editor*
Miles Cowsill
*Photography*
Miles Cowsill and Wales Tourist Board

First published by Lily Publications 1994
Second (Premier Guide) edition 1996

*Front Cover*: Rhossili Bay
*Back cover*: Oxwich

Copyright © 1996 Lily Publications. All rights reserved. Any reproduction in whole or part is strictly prohibited. The content contained herein is based on the best available information at the time of research. The publishers assume no liability whatsoever arising from the publishing of material contained herein.

All accommodation participates in the Wales Tourist Board's inspection scheme. If readers have any concern about standards of accommodation, please take the matter up direct with the provider of the accommodation as soon as possible. Failing satisfaction, please contact the Wales Tourist Board, Development Services Unit, 2 Fitzalan Road, Cardiff CF2 1UY. Published by Lily Publications, PO Box 9, Narberth, Pembrokeshire SA68 0YT, Wales. Tel: (01834) 891461. Fax: (01834) 891463. ISBN 1 899602 20 8.

# Contents

New Discoveries At Every Turn . . . . . . . . . . . . . . . . 3
The Great Beach Holiday . . . . . . . . . . . . . . . . . . . . 4
Llanelli's Golden Coast . . . . . . . . . . . . . . . . . . . . . 9
Swansea Bay & Mumbles . . . . . . . . . . . . . . . . . . . 17
The Gower Peninsula . . . . . . . . . . . . . . . . . . . . . . 38
The Vale of Neath . . . . . . . . . . . . . . . . . . . . . . . . 49
Port Talbot & the Afan Valley . . . . . . . . . . . . . . . . 55
Porthcawl & Ogwr . . . . . . . . . . . . . . . . . . . . . . . . 60
The Great Sporting & Activity Holiday . . . . . . . . 63
Exploring Carmarthenshire . . . . . . . . . . . . . . . . . 67
Tourist Information Centres . . . . . . . . . . . . . . . . 69
Accommodation & Eating Out . . . . . . . . . . . . . . 70
Acknowledgements . . . . . . . . . . . . . . . . . . . . . . 72
Index . . . . . . . . . . . . . . . . . . . . . . . . . . . . . . . . 72

## MAPS

Llanelli . . . . . . . . . . . . . . . . . . . . . . . . . . . . . . . . 9
Swansea city centre . . . . . . . . . . . . . . . . . . . . . 18
Swansea Bay & area . . . . . . . . . . . . . . . . . . . . 36
Port Talbot . . . . . . . . . . . . . . . . . . . . . . . . . . . 55
Porthcawl . . . . . . . . . . . . . . . . . . . . . . . . . . . . 60

## New Discoveries at Every Turn

This comprehensive visitor guide, first published in 1994, has been completely revised and updated for this new *Premier Guide* edition. It is the only publication to embrace in one volume six distinctive but adjoining holiday areas of south-west Wales – from the golden sands of Llanelli on the Loughor estuary in the west to the Heritage Coast beaches of Ogmore-by-Sea and Southerndown in the east.

This stretch of South Wales coastline takes in Gower, Swansea Bay and Porthcawl, each long established among Britain's most popular seaside destinations. Some readers, however, will no doubt be surprised to discover that places traditionally associated with industry and coal mining also have a great deal to offer and are making a big impact on the tourist map. Valleys and shoreline devastated by such activity have been painstakingly reclaimed and great efforts made to restore their natural beauty.

Hence every turn of these pages provides more than a few pleasant surprises. The delights awaiting you include superb beaches, magnificent coastlines, enchanting waterfalls, medieval castles, estuaries teeming with wildlife, vast country parks, first-class sports and leisure facilities, Swansea's excellent shopping centre and marina, and holiday attractions of every description.

For those visitors who wish to explore a little further afield, this guide also gives a fleeting impression of Carmarthenshire.

*Worms Head*

Other areas bordering south-west Wales are covered in further *Premier Guides*, notably *The Premier Guide to Pembrokeshire*, *The Premier Guide to Brecon Beacons & The Heart of Wales*, and *The Premier Guide to Cardiff*. All are available from branches of WH Smith and other leading retailers, or direct from Lily Publications at the address shown on the title page.

I hope that you will find this guide both interesting and useful – and that your holiday in this beautiful part of Wales is a happy and memorable one.

Miles Cowsill,
Managing Director,
Lily Publications

# The Great Beach Holiday

The South Wales coastline described in this guide boasts an abundance of superb beaches. In fact, there are all kinds of beaches for all kinds of people.

Wide, safe, sandy beaches for children and families. Secluded, quiet coves and small bays where you can bask in the solitude. And beaches for surfers, windsurfers, water-skiers, canoeists and sailing enthusiasts.

Regular tests are carried out to ensure that bathing water quality around the most popular and accessible beaches meets at least the EC minimum standard. Some beaches are also declared dog-free zones during summer months for reasons of safety and hygiene.

The following is a quick guide to the region's beaches, 7 of which won important Seaside Awards in 1996. These awards are administered by the Tidy Britain Group, an independent national charity, and are given on the basis of beach cleanliness, hygiene, safety and environmental management.

Some of the facilities described here are applicable during the summer season only – in particular lifeguard patrols, regular bus services and beach shops and cafes.

*Caswell Bay*

## CEFN SIDAN SANDS, PEMBREY

This is a truly magnificent stretch of golden sands – 8 miles in all, including the southern extension of Pembrey beach – and in 1996 it won a Resort Seaside Award from the Tidy Britain Group. Over recent years it has also been a regular winner of the prestigious European Blue Flag Award. The beach is backed by dunes and the attractive conservation area of Pembrey Country Park, which offers nature trails, walks, picnics, cafes and restaurant, and a host of sports and activities such as the dry ski slope. The beach, which is safe for swimming and good for surfing, is well monitored by the park's ranger service, and in summer there is also a lifeguard patrol. As with the beach at Pembrey, the facilities here are equal to those of an established seaside resort because of the very extensive amenities and attractions of the country park.

## PEMBREY

The beach at Pembrey, accessible through the country park, is a southern extension of award-winning Cefn Sidan Sands, which curve round towards Burry Port. Treacherous currents make bathing unsafe at the mouth of the Loughor estuary. There is a golf course set in the sand dunes nearby, and Burry Port itself has a launching slipway and harbour and is popular with boating enthusiasts. Facilities are extensive because of the proximity of Pembrey Country Park.

## LLANELLI

Llanelli beach comes as a pleasant surprise to first-time visitors. It is a long beach with superb views over the Loughor estuary and the northern shoreline of Gower, and at low tide there is a vast stretch of exposed sand. Facilities: easy but limited parking, easy access to the beach.

## SWANSEA BAY

Miles of wide sands stretch from the Maritime Quarter to the Mumbles, backed by all the leisure, sports and shopping amenities of Wales' second largest city. The bay is used mainly for recreational purposes – such as windsurfing, fishing, canoeing, sailing and water-skiing – rather than for bathing. Parts of the beach are designated dog-free zones during the summer. Facilities: toilets, regular bus service, parking, shops along the promenade, easy access.

## THE MUMBLES

Standing at the western tip of the wide sweep of Swansea Bay, Mumbles has a long promenade, a Victorian pier with a small fun fair and amusements, Mumbles Head lighthouse, and the famous Mumbles Mile of shops, pubs and restaurants. The beach is popular for recreation and watersports. Other facilities: toilets, regular bus service, parking, deck chair hire, launching slipways, easy access.

## BRACELET BAY, GOWER

A small cove with pebbles and rock pools. Popular for canoeing, fishing, walking and Mumbles Hill Local Nature Reserve. There is a beach shop cafe at nearby Limeslade Bay. Facilities: lifeguard patrol, toilets (abled and disabled), telephone, regular bus service, parking, steps to beach.

## LIMESLADE BAY, GOWER

A rocky cove with sand exposed at low tide. Popular for fishing and swimming. Rescue Aids are sited on the beach. Other facilities: toilets (abled and disabled), regular bus service, parking, beach shop, steps to beach.

## ROTHERSLADE & LANGLAND, GOWER

Though part of the same bay, these two beaches are separated at high tide, Langland being the larger and very popular with families. At low tide there is a fine stretch of sandy beach, fringed by beach huts. The bay is a popular venue for golf and tennis as well as for swimming, surfing and fishing. Both beaches are designated dog-free zones during summer months, and Langland is a popular surfing beach. Facilities: lifeguard patrol, toilets (abled and disabled), telephone, regular bus service, parking, beach shops and cafes, deckchair hire, steps to beaches.

## CASWELL BAY, GOWER

A large and popular sandy beach, well patronised by families, and set in a very picturesque bay. An added attraction is Bishop's Wood Nature Reserve in Caswell Valley. The beach is ideal for swimming, surfing, windsurfing, fishing and canoeing, and is a dog-free zone in summer. In 1996 it won a Rural Beach Seaside Award from the Tidy Britain Group. Facilities: deckchair hire, toilets, telephone, regular bus service, parking, beach shop, easy access.

## BRANDY COVE, GOWER

A secluded sandy cove with rocks and pebbles, once notorious for smuggling. This is a good beach for swimming and fishing, but its isolated location means a long walk from the main road. Facilities: regular bus service, shops in Bishopston village.

## PWLL-DU BAY, GOWER

A large, secluded sandy beach backed by a high bank of pebbles, through which a stream from the beautiful Bishopston Valley enters the sea. There is a long walk to this isolated beach from the main road, but once here you can enjoy good swimming and fishing. Facilities: regular bus service, shops in Bishopston village.

## PEBBLES BAY, GOWER

This pebble and sand beach, which is covered at high tide, is also in an isolated spot and can only be reached after a long walk from the main road. Facilities: regular bus service to the villages of Southgate and Parkmill, which offer shops and parking.

## TOR BAY, GOWER

A sandy beach lying west of the Great Tor rock at the eastern end of Oxwich Bay. Facilities: regular bus service to the nearest village of Penmaen, which also offers limited parking, but the walk to the beach is long and difficult and access is down a steep path.

## PENMAEN SANDS, GOWER

As with Tor Bay, access to Penmaen Sands involves a long walk and steep descent. The reward is that this sandy beach, located to the west of Three Cliffs Bay, is very often deserted. Close by are several historic sites, including the remains of Penmaen Old Castle, a megalithic tomb and a church. According to legend a lost village lies buried beneath the sands.

Facilities: regular bus service to Penmaen, where there is also limited parking.

### THREE CLIFFS BAY, GOWER

One of the most picturesque bays on the Gower Peninsula, with spectacular views. The ruins of Pennard Castle overlook the valley, down which a tidal stream runs into the sea, creating dangerous currents. Facilities: telephone, regular bus services to the villages of Southgate and Parkmill (which also have shops and parking), and access to the beach only after a long walk from either village.

### CRAWLEY, GOWER

Another isolated beach which can only be reached after a long walk from Nicholaston Cross, to which there is a regular bus service.

### OXWICH BAY, GOWER

One of the most popular family beaches on Gower, with a long stretch of golden sand. In summer there are guided walks through the Nature Reserve. Within the reserve are most of the dunes, marshes and woods skirting Oxwich Sands. This is also a popular venue for sailing, water-skiing, fishing and canoeing, and windsurfing tuition and hire are available. In 1996 Oxwich Bay won a Rural Beach Seaside Award from the Tidy Britain Group. Facilities: boat slip, toilets, regular bus service, parking, beach shops and cafes, and easy access.

### HORTON, GOWER

A sandy beach sheltered by the huge sand dunes which link it to Port Eynon. Horton is a popular spot for watersports and fishing, and there are lifeguards at Port Eynon. Facilities: toilets (abled and disabled), regular bus service, parking, shops near beach, easy access.

### PORT EYNON, GOWER

Port Eynon is one of the star attractions of Gower, with a large sandy beach and excellent facilities. In 1996 it won a Rural Beach Seaside Award from the Tidy Britain Group. The beach is very popular for windsurfing, canoeing and boating. Facilities: lifeguard patrol, youth hostel, toilets (abled and disabled), regular bus service, parking, beach shops and cafes, windsurfing hire, boat slip, and easy access.

### MEWSLADE BAY, GOWER

A secluded and isolated sandy beach set amongst magnificent cliff scenery west of Thurba Head. Facilities: regular bus service to Pitton or parking in a private farm field, but access to the beach requires a long though pleasant walk.

### FALL BAY, GOWER

An extension of Mewslade Bay, this secluded sandy beach is covered at high tide. Its isolated location south of Rhossili means that access is only possible after a long walk.

### RHOSSILI BAY, GOWER

Considered by many to be one of the finest beaches in Wales, if not Britain, Rhossili and adjoining Llangennith won a Rural Beach Seaside Award from the Tidy Britain Group in 1996. The village of Rhossili is dramatically poised on a cliff 200 feet above the superb crescent of sand, with magnificent views over the outstretched finger of the Worms Head peninsula and the huge sweep of Carmarthen Bay to the west. The beach offers excellent bathing and is also very popular for surfing, canoeing, hang-gliding and fishing. Access to Worms Head is restricted to about two hours either side of low tide. Facilities: National Trust shop and Information Centre, toilets (abled and disabled), a regular bus service, large private car park, and shops in Rhossili village. Access to the beach is via a long steep walk from the village.

### LLANGENNITH, GOWER

An extension of Rhossili Bay (with which it shared a Rural Beach Seaside Award in 1996), Llangennith is acknowledged as one of Britain's premier surfing beaches and is a favourite spot for swimming, canoeing and fishing. At low tide you can cross the sand to the island of Burry Holms and discover the remains of a medieval monastic settlement. Away from the beach, the village of Llangennith also attracts visitors, and the well-known Gower folk singer Phil Tanner is buried in the churchyard here. Beach facilities: toilets, bus service, large private car park, shops on the caravan site in the village, easy access to the beach.

### BLUEPOOL BAY, GOWER

A sandy cove accessible only on foot from Llangennith or Broughton Bay. The bay is a dangerous bathing area and gets its name from the

*Three Cliffs Bay*

circular rock pool at the foot of the cliffs, in which bathing is not recommended either. Facilities: regular bus service to Llangennith and parking at Broughton Bay, but access to the beach is extremely difficult.

### BROUGHTON BAY, GOWER

Fringed by the sand dunes of Broughton Burrows, this large sandy beach runs into Whiteford Sands towards the mouth of the Loughor estuary. The treacherous currents of the estuary mean that bathing here is dangerous both at low water mark and on the outgoing tide, but by way of compensation the cliff-top views are dramatic. Facilities: bus service to Llangennith, where there is a private car park and a caravan site offering shops, toilets and easy access to the beach.

### WHITEFORD SANDS, GOWER

This beautiful sandy beach extends to Whiteford Point – the most northerly point on Gower and the site of a disused lighthouse. The beach is backed by Whiteford Burrows and together they form part of a National Nature Reserve. As with the adjacent beach of Broughton Bay, bathing here is dangerous because of treacherous estuary currents. Facilities: bus service to Llanmadoc, with easy access to the beach from the caravan site.

### ABERAVON, PORT TALBOT

Two miles of sands, a promenade and the sports and leisure facilities of Afon Lido have made Aberavon a popular destination for day trippers over the years. Now a major redevelopment of the entire Aberavon seafront is under way. Facilities: promenade with children's play areas, emergency telephone, lifeguard patrol, regular bus service to Port Talbot, free parking, toilets (abled and disabled), local shops plus shopping in Port Talbot (1 mile away), easy beach access.

### MARGAM SANDS, PORT TALBOT

A large expanse of sand lying to the south of Port Talbot docks and backed by the dunes of Margam Burrows and the less welcome spread of Port Talbot's infamous steelworks. The proximity of the works has tended to overshadow the fact that Margam is a superb beach, stretching south for several miles and running into Kenfig Sands and burrows. To the east are all the attractions and picturesque scenery of Margam Country Park.

### REST BAY, PORTHCAWL

A small bay which at low tide boasts an inviting expanse of clean golden sand and several rock pools. The beach is very popular with surfers, and lifeguards are on duty during the peak summer months. Superb cliff-top walks are an added attraction. In 1996 Rest Bay won a Rural Beach Seaside Award from the Tidy Britain Group. Facilities nearby include all the amenities and attractions of the lively summer resort of Porthcawl, which boasts a new promenade and other improvements.

### SANDY BAY AND TRECCO BAY

These two beaches, with wide expanses of safe golden sands and an abundance of rock pools, are very popular with families. Each also has a caravan park sited adjacent to the beach, and nearby are all the resort amenities of Porthcawl itself and the fun and attractions of Coney Beach Pleasure Park. The beaches offer safe bathing and are patrolled by lifeguards in the summer season.

### MERTHYR MAWR, PORTHCAWL

A haven of peace and tranquility, this is an area of high grassy sand dunes rather than beach, though it does extend between low hills and the sea. A designated SSSI – Site of Special Scientific Interest.

### OGMORE-BY-SEA, NEAR PORTHCAWL

Attractively located at the mouth of the River Ogmore, the sandy beach is fringed with areas of grass. However, estuary currents make bathing here dangerous. Facilities include easy parking near the shore, and cafes.

### SOUTHERNDOWN, NEAR OGMORE

A popular surfing bay, Southerndown lies on the Glamorgan Heritage Coast. At low tide there is a wide expanse of clean golden sand and an abundance of rock pools. Fine views are enhanced by cliff-top walks. Facilities: limited parking, lifeguards, Heritage Coast Visitor Centre. In 1996 Southerndown won a Rural Beach Seaside Award from the Tidy Britain Group.

# Llanelli's Golden Coast

For a town which was once the tinplate capital of the world, and whose prosperity has been forged from the spoils of heavy industry, Llanelli comes as a pleasant surprise to the first-time visitor.

It stands on the beautiful Loughor estuary, on the eastern seaboard of Carmarthen Bay, within easy reach of many attractions. Among these are magnificent Cefn Sidan Sands and Pembrey Country Park, award-winning Penclacwydd Wildfowl & Wetlands Centre, Pembrey Motorsports Centre, Kidwelly Castle, the spectacular beaches and scenery of the Gower Peninsula, and the excellent shopping, leisure and entertainment facilities of Swansea.

Though home to a population of over 35,000 people, Llanelli enjoys the same relaxing pace of life as many smaller seaside resorts. The attractive pedestrianised shopping centre, refurbished in 1994, has many familiar High Street names and a good choice of places to eat. There is also a bustling daily indoor market and a twice-weekly open air market. Construction work is now in hand on a major extension of the town's retail centre.

One of Llanelli's other pleasant surprises is the spread of attractive parks and gardens. Sandy Water Park, People's Park, Parc Howard and other places offer relaxation in very pleasant surroundings. On the other hand, if excitement is your craving, there's one park you really shouldn't miss – Stradey Park, home of Llanelli Rugby Football Club, on a Saturday afternoon. The Scarlets are one of Britain's most successful club sides and a familiar name to rugby fans around the world. The club's rugby posts are adorned with saucepans – a tribute to the boisterous local anthem "Sospan Fach" (The Little Saucepan) which was Llanelli's trademark. Stradey Park also has a museum depicting the history of the club, and it is open to visitors by arrangement.

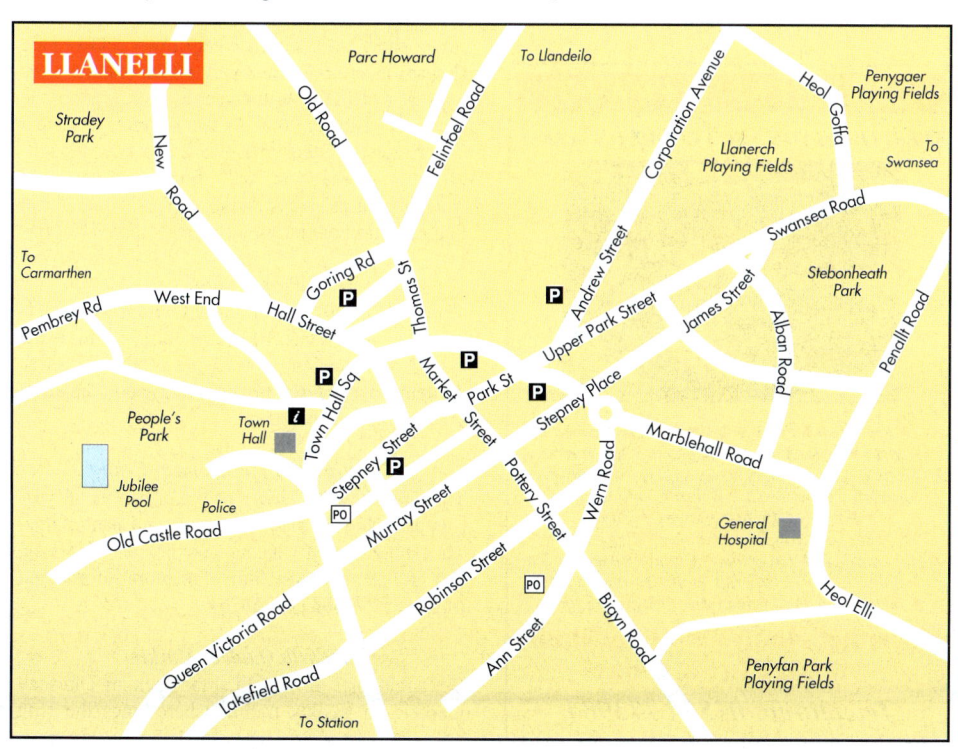

For those who prefer to participate rather than spectate, Llanelli offers impressive sports facilities – not least the superb new indoor complex of Llanelli Leisure Centre.

But the town's biggest surprise is its beach and coastline. The acres of industrial dereliction and mountains of waste which for years plagued the neglected area of South Llanelli have been swept away in the wake of an ambitious multi-million pound scheme, including a major coast protection and enhancement programme. The result is a stunning shoreline backed by landscaped parkland, picturesque water features and a 3-mile promenade. At low tide the long beach, frequented by oystercatchers and curlews, reveals a vast area of sand and saltmarsh that seems to stretch right across the Loughor estuary to the beckoning Gower Peninsula. Views over the estuary, and along the near coastline towards Burry Port and Pembrey, are superb.

### New iron age prosperity

Like much of South Wales today, Llanelli has undergone a metamorphosis as traditional industries have faded away and leisure and tourism have blossomed.

Such a transition is nothing new in the town's history. Though coal was mined in Llanelli and Kidwelly as early as 1536, Llanelli was still only a village until the mid-18th century. Yet within a hundred years it was transformed by the sudden and rapid development of the iron industry. Early in the 19th century, Alexander Raby opened the Furnace ironworks north of the town, and followed this by building the first modern dock and the Dafen works, which opened in 1847. The harbour was a hive of activity as iron, coal, tinplate and then steel production flourished. Chimneys shaped the skyline and many small tinplate works prospered in the hands of craftsmen – a story retold in the Tinplate Industry Museum at Trostre and in the museum at Parc Howard. The latter also contains examples of Llanelli pottery, for which the town was famous between 1840 and 1925.

Llanelli has other modest claims to fame. The home of two breweries – Felinfoel and Buckleys – the town was the first to put beer into cans. Another local innovation was the spare wheel, patented by a Llanelli family. And Llanelli had the first Welsh language school and the first music library.

### Parc Howard

Just a short walk from Llanelli town centre, Parc Howard is an ornamental park which features trees unusual to Britain. In the centre of the park is the Mansion House, the former home of local benefactor Sir Stafford Howard and now Llanelli Museum. Here you will find an interesting collection of paintings and examples of early local tinplate. For more information ring 01554 741100.

### People's Park

The park, to the rear of Llanell's impressive neo-Jacobean Town Hall (100 years old in 1996), is the site of the excellent new leisure centre, attractive gardens, a playground, paddling pool, bowling green and tennis courts.

### Theatre Elli Entertainment Centre

This hosts a wide variety of performances all year round, including plays, musicals and pantomime. The Three Screen Cinema Complex shows classic hits and all the latest films. For more information ring 01554 774057 or 759764.

### Llanelli Outdoor Market

Get a real taste of Llanelli at the open air Thursday market – a weekly tradition here since the 15th

---

## LLANELLI MARKET
**EVERYTHING YOU NEED UNDER ONE ROOF**

- Fresh fish • Fruit & veg • Flowers • Bread
- Meat • Cooked meats • Seafood & laverbread
- Sweets & confectionery • Newsagents • Hardware
- Speciality delicatesen • Wools • Toys & games
- Fabrics • Picture framing • Cards
- Records & tapes • Antiques • Petfoods
- Haberdashery • Ice cream • China • Dried flowers
- Baby wear • Welsh craft shop • Leather goods
- Jewellery repairs • Lingerie • Electrical goods

**Opening Hours: 9am - 5.30pm
Monday to Saturday
Telephone: 01554 773984**

century. Among the many things on offer is a very tempting choice of fresh local produce, including fish, cockles, vegetables, Welsh cheeses, laver bread and other delicacies. The market, also open on Saturdays, is in addition to the daily indoor market.

### Sandy Water Park
Once the site of a huge steelworks, the park offers views over Carmarthen Bay and Gower. Centre of attraction is a 16-acre lake and its many opportunities for watersports. There are also pleasant landscaped walkways with access to Llanelli beach.

### Swiss Valley
Swiss Valley is the beautiful area around the Upper and Lower Lliedi reservoirs, just to the north of Llanelli. Woodland walks, wildlife, trout fishing and relaxation are the big attractions here.

### The Furnace & Pond
Just north of Llanelli is the village of Furnace – named after the 19th-century iron furnace which worked round the clock to produce cannon and cannon balls for the Napoleonic wars. Nearby, on the site of the old Trebeddrod Reservoir, is the recently-developed leisure area of Furnace Pond. Here you can enjoy country walks, a nature trail, fishing and a stroll through the landscaped Japanese water garden.

### Penclacwydd Wildfowl & Wetlands Centre
Which migrating swan is capable of flying as high as Everest in temperatures as low as minus 48° C? Why are flamingos pink, and why do they stand on one leg? Exactly how deep can a diving duck dive?

The answers to such questions can be found at this award-winning Centre a few miles east of Llanelli. It opened in 1991 and is the only one of its kind in Wales. It was designed by Sir Peter Scott and built by LLanelli Borough Council, who lease it to the Wildfowl & Wetlands Trust.

Popular with experts and sightseers alike, Penclacwydd is beautifully landscaped and is situated on the Loughor estuary. Two hundred acres of saltmarsh, watermeadow and estuary provide home to large numbers of wintering ducks and waders, which are best seen from the purpose-built hides. The views are spectacular as flocks of curlew, oystercatcher and redshank wheel over the saltmarsh.

The Centre has a resident population of more than 1100 wildfowl originating from all over the world. These include black-necked swans, the rare and endangered white-winged wood duck, and Caribbean flamingos. Small birds of prey are seen here too, such as peregrine falcons, kestrels and short-eared owls, along with herons and kingfishers.

All admission money goes directly to conserving wetland environments. The Centre has excellent facilities for both able-bodied and disabled visitors, with easy paths for pushchairs, wheelchair access to most areas – including the hides – and free parking. There is also a gift and book shop, a coffee shop/cafe and a Visitor Centre.

You can round off your visit by becoming a member of the Wildfowl & Wetlands Trust, or even adopting a duck or a swan. The Centre is open all year round and offers low-price family tickets. It is 3 miles east of Llanelli, just off the A484 Swansea road. From the M4 take junction 47 or 48. For more information ring 01554 741087, or see advertisement on Page 13.

## *The Stradey Park*

Splendidly situated on a hill overlooking Llanelli towards Carmarthen Bay, The Stradey Park is built around a 19th Century crenellated house and offers the warmth of our traditional Welsh hospitality and friendliness.

Llanelli and its Golden Coast are ideally situated to explore the scenic and historic wonders of beautiful South and West Wales. Golden beaches, country parks, historic castles, The Wildfowl and Wetlands Trust Centre, and Pembrey race circuit, are just some of the many attractions making Llanelli the ideal place to stay.

Telephone Anne, Alison or Helen for further details of our Bargain Break Holidays, open throughout the year. All 80 bedrooms have private bathroom, colour television, tea & coffee making facilities and direct dial telephones.

**FORTE** HOTELS

Furnace, Llanelli, Dyfed SA15 4HA
Telephone: 01554 758171 Fax: 01554 777974

# Pembrey Circuit

## If you prefer to live in the fast lane, why not sample the thrills and spills of motorsport at Pembrey Circuit

The Pembrey Circuit was taken over by the British Automobile Racing Circuit in 1990, it was upgraded in 1992 to achieve British Formula 3 and British Touring Car status.

The circuit is located in 500 acres of land combining a variety of grass, concrete and tarmac surfaces making it suitable for all types of motorsport. The 1.5 mile main circuit consists of a perfect combination of curves and straights to provide a challenge to all comers.

The wide run off areas ensure that the majority of driver/rider errors do no serious damage to man or machine and provide the spectator with additional entertainment. however, it must be remembered that motorsport is hazardous and extra care must be taken whilst at the centre.

During week days the circuit is open for general motorcycle and car testing as well as for corporate entertainment. Also, many of the Top Formula 1 Teams including Williams, Renault, Bennetton, Ford and McLaren us the facility for test and development work.

The annual Welsh Festival of Motorsport held each September gives everybody the opportunity to sample motorsport at little or no cost. It includes a full programme of motorsports combined with a motorshow and various stalls and entertainments around the perimeter providing good family fun.

Race meetings are held most weekends between March and October and include Modern, Classic and Vintage motorcycles; Modern, Classic and Vintage Cars; Rallycross, Tarmac Rallies, Karting as well as an array of Championship Events.

The Formula One Bar and Restaurant is popular with spectator and competitor alike, serving hot and cold food and refreshments throughout race days.

**Pembrey Circuit • Welsh Sports Centre • Pembrey • Llanelli SA16 0HZ**
**Telephone 01654 891042**

*Llanelli's Golden Coast*

## Pembrey & Burry Port

To the west of Llanelli, the area around Pembrey and Burry Port is very well known for three of the region's major tourist attractions – Pembrey Country Park, Cefn Sidan Sands and the Welsh Motorsports Centre.

On an historic note, Burry Port is remembered as the place where the waterproof material used in the making of the Mackintosh was discovered by chance at the town's copperworks, when a piece of green baize from a worker's apron accidentally fell into a vat and became waterproofed during the coppermaking process! And on 18th June 1928 the seaplane *Friendship* splashed down near the harbour after a 23-hour flight, thus becoming the first aircraft to make a non-stop crossing of the Atlantic. Its passenger, Amelia Earhart, simultaneously became the first woman to make the crossing by air. Memorials to this historic event can be seen in Burry Port harbour and the George Inn, in Stepney Road.

### Burry Port Harbour

Built in the days when the coal and tinplate industries were thriving, the harbour is now well patronised by yachts, pleasure craft and fishermen. The annual Fishing Festival attracts anglers from all over the UK and offers excellent prizes and entertainment.

### St. Illtyd's Church, Pembrey

The 13th-century church is the oldest building in the area, and in the churchyard is a memorial to those who drowned when the French ship *Jeune Emma* ran aground on the treacherous Cefn Sidan Sands in 1828. Among the victims was Adeline Coqueline, who according to the inscription was "the niece of Josephine, Consort to the renowned individual Napoleon Bonaparte". Outside the church gates is a circle of stones attached to the church wall – a rare example of a medieval animal pound, where stray animals were impounded and eventually sold off to swell church funds if no one claimed them.

### Pembrey Country Park

Owned and managed by the local authority, this top tourist attraction is a wonderful blend of coast and

---

**THE WILDFOWL & WETLANDS TRUST, LLANELLI**

After wandering leisurely around the grounds following the hundreds of ducks, geese and swans, return to the Visitor Centre where the fun has only just begun.

The Visitor Centre is custom built with children of all ages in mind, if you are 6 or 60 there is something for you.

Access from A484 one mile west of Loughor.
*(Follow the brown duck signs)*
**Tel: (01554) 741087**
**Open all year round**
The Wildfowl & Wetlands Trust, Penclacwydd, Llwynhendy, Llanelli, Carmarthenshire SA14 9SH

---

## Shoreline
### Leisure Home Park

*Shoreline* is a first class Holiday Park, where the majority of caravans and chalets are privately owned. There are also fully equipped, 6-8 berth chalets and caravans for hire and for sale. *Shoreline* is between Bury Port Boat Marina and 5 miles of golden sands at Cefn Sidan beach. Various sporting activities are available locally. Llanelli's shops, Leisure Centre, theatre and cinema are only four miles away.

**Burry Port, Nr. Llanelli, Dyfed SA16 0HD**
**Telephone: (01554) 832657**

## PEMBREY COUNTRY PARK

**Open daily from dawn to dusk.
Over 500 acres of glorious parkland
and 7 miles of golden sands and dunes**

Attractions include:-
- Pitch and Putt Golf
- Narrow Gauge Railway
- Visitor Centre & Gift Shop
- Large Adventure Playground
- Orienteering Course
- Childrens entertainment daily during schools Summer Holidays
- Nature Trails and Picnic Sites
- Dry Ski Slope and Cafe
- Toboggan Run
- Cycle Hire
- Equestrian Centre
- Restaurant and Beach Cafe
- 'Easy Rider' available for disabled

N.B. Main attractions subject to seasonal opening

*For further information Tel:- Pembrey Country Park, (01554) 833913
Ski slope :- (01554) 834443
Located off A484 Llanelli to Carmarthen Coast Road, just outside Burry Port.
Follow the brown signs*

## LLYN LLECH OWAIN COUNTRY PARK

**Llyn Llech Owain
Country Park,
Gorslas, Near Cross Hands**

*This splendid country park opened to the public in 1994 after sensitive development by Carmarthen District Council. Its beauty lies in its simplicity, drawing on the natural environment of the parks' 158 acres of conifer woodland and 10 acre lake.*

*Visitor Centre, nature trails, boardwalks, mountain bike trail, play area, etc.
New for '96 - Cafeteria.
Contact the Park Ranger on*
**(01269) 832229**

## PARC GWLEDIG GELLI AUR COUNTRY PARK

PARC
GWLEDIG
**GELLI
AUR**
COUNTRY
PARK

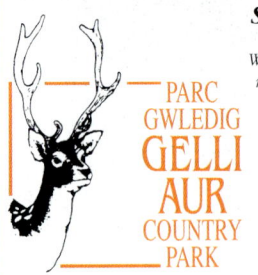

**See the Deer at Gelli Aur.......**

*Wooded parkland surrounding a magnificent mansion. Situated 3 miles west of Llandeilo, just off the B4300.*

- *Visitor Centre and Cafeteria*
- *Arboretum and Terrace Gardens*
- *Deer Park*
- *Nature Trails*
- *Childrens Play Area*
- *Events, Guided Walks and Craft Demonstrations*

*The Country Park is open all year*

*Tel: Dryslwyn (01558) 668885*

countryside. It occupies the site of the old Pembrey Royal Ordnance Factory. There are over 500 acres of beautiful woods and grassland, fringed by one of the finest beaches in Europe – Cefn Sidan Sands. There is no admission charge to the park; you pay only for parking. It is open all year round from dawn till dusk, and the facilities and attractions are first-class, including the dry ski slope and the Cobra toboggan run – the longest in Wales. For further information ring 01554 833913.

### The Welsh Motorsports Centre
The roar of the race track and the dash for the chequered flag never fail to enthral the crowds at Pembrey's famous motorsport venue. Set in 500 acres, the challenging circuit regularly hosts top competitive action on both two wheels and four, and is one of the leading motorsport attractions in Britain. For more information ring 01554 891042.

## Kidwelly

Kidwelly is an ancient town standing at the confluence of the rivers Gwendraeth Fach and Gwendraeth Fawr, which run out into the sandy Tywi estuary of Carmarthen Bay.

The town received its first charter under Henry I and is therefore one of the oldest boroughs in Wales. Indeed, many of the visitors who come here are drawn by Kidwelly's medieval castle, which is remarkably well preserved and stands imposingly on a steep ridge above the river.

The town grew up around the castle and was also fortified. Though no other original town buildings survive, Kidwelly still retains something of a medieval air by virtue of the 14th-century bridge across the river and the ancient church of St. Mary the Virgin, impressive for its tall spire.

In much more recent times, Kidwelly was a busy trading port and in the 19th century was firmly established as one of Britain's largest tinplate manufacturing centres. This achievement is proudly recorded in the fascinating industrial museum, which occupies the site of the old Kidwelly Tinplate Works.

### Kidwelly Castle
The original motte and bailey castle, made of earth and timber, was built in about 1106 by Bishop Roger of Salisbury, under the sovereignty of Henry I. It was rebuilt in stone in the late 13th and early 14th centuries largely in the form in which we see it today, though there were some later medieval and Tudor additions. The castle was one of a long line of Norman fortresses which stretched west to St. Bride's Bay on the Pembrokeshire coastline. Repeatedly attacked and captured by the Welsh in its early years, the castle was strengthened by means of the concentric method of defence – building walls within walls – and is one of the finest surviving examples of this type of medieval military architecture. Much of the castle still stands today, since it played no part in the Civil Wars and therefore escaped the damaging attentions of Cromwell.

### Kidwelly Industrial Museum
The museum was officially opened in 1988 and is the only place in Wales where you can see how tinplate was made by hand. It is situated on the banks of the Gwendraeth Fach river, on the former site of the Kidwelly Tinplate Works, which ceased production in 1941, and the 164-foot chimney stack rising high above the valley provides an unmistakeable landmark. The museum also provides an insight into the history of the local coal industry. Among the many fascinating items to be seen here are waterwheels, industrial steam and diesel locomotives, and even a typesetting machine from the local newspaper, the *Star*.

### Kidwelly Quay
Here you will find one of the first canals to be built in Wales. Recently restored, it provides a superb picnic area and serves as a reminder of the days when Kidwelly was a thriving port.

### St. Mary's Church
Once the church of the Benedictine Priory, it is notable for its spire, which was a later addition to the 13th-century tower. Inside the church is a 14th-century alabaster statue of the Virgin and Child.

# Naturally Beautiful
## *Swansea*

*Swansea, Mumbles & Gower*, the naturally beautiful gateway of West Wales. Beautiful sandy beaches, pretty villages, glorious parks, boats sailing across the bay, wild ponies running over moorland. Need we say more?

For a FREE brochure or further information:
call: Freephone 0800 521811 or fax: 01792 464602

CITY AND COUNTY OF SWANSEA
DINAS A SIR ABERTAWE

# Swansea Bay & Mumbles

Granted city status in 1969 with the Investiture of Prince Charles as Prince of Wales, Swansea today is a thriving regional capital. It is a university city and a centre for shopping, recreation, leisure, commerce and administration. And it is a city by the sea, frequented by day trippers and holidaymakers wishing to experience all the attractions and delights of Swansea Bay, Mumbles and the Gower Peninsula.

Packed into this corner of south-west Wales is a very satisfying mix of magnificent beaches and scenery, great family attractions and entertainment, first-class leisure and sports facilities, a wide choice of accommodation, and a wonderful sense of Welsh history and culture.

Swansea is also the birthplace of the great poet and writer Dylan Thomas, who was born in the Uplands district of the city in 1914 and died in New York in November 1953. The Dylan Thomas Theatre is one of the star attractions of Swansea's award-winning Maritime Quarter, which has brought new life and purpose to derelict dockland.

### Swansea in history

Swansea has a very chequered history, to say the least. It was founded by the Vikings, developed into a busy administrative and trading centre by the Normans, established as a prosperous industrial and seaside town by the Victorians, and flattened by the bombs of the Luftwaffe.

Many of the early settlements which grew around the coastlines of West Wales regularly fell victim to marauding Vikings, who robbed churches of their riches and torched villages and homesteads. But as well as destroying communities, the Vikings also created them. Swansea is a case in point. The name derives from *Sweyn's ey* (meaning inlet or island) – a possible reference to Swein Forkbeard. He was King of Denmark from 986 to 1014, and it is known that he visited the Bristol Channel.

Artefacts on show in Swansea Museum prove that the Romans also occupied the area. But it was the Normans who brought order and prosperity, first building a castle and then developing the town of Swansea around it. A busy centre of administration and trade, it was granted several royal charters and soon had town walls, a church, a thriving harbour, a weekly market and regular fairs. A few miles away, at Oystermouth, a second castle was built.

*Swansea Marina*

Much of this good work was undone by Owain Glyndwr in the period of Welsh revolt between 1400 and 1410, when the town and castle of Swansea were seized and laid to ruin.

Yet in time the town not only recovered but achieved a position as a major port and industrial centre. It was coal, discovered in seams close to the surface in the land around Swansea Bay, which provided a great export opportunity.

These same deposits also enabled Swansea to become one of the world's most important centres for the manufacture of metal during the 18th and 19th centuries. In 1716 a copper works was established here. The abundance of coal gave rise to others and by the end of the 19th century all but one of the copper works in Britain were to be found in the Swansea area.

The production of nickel, zinc, tinplate and steel

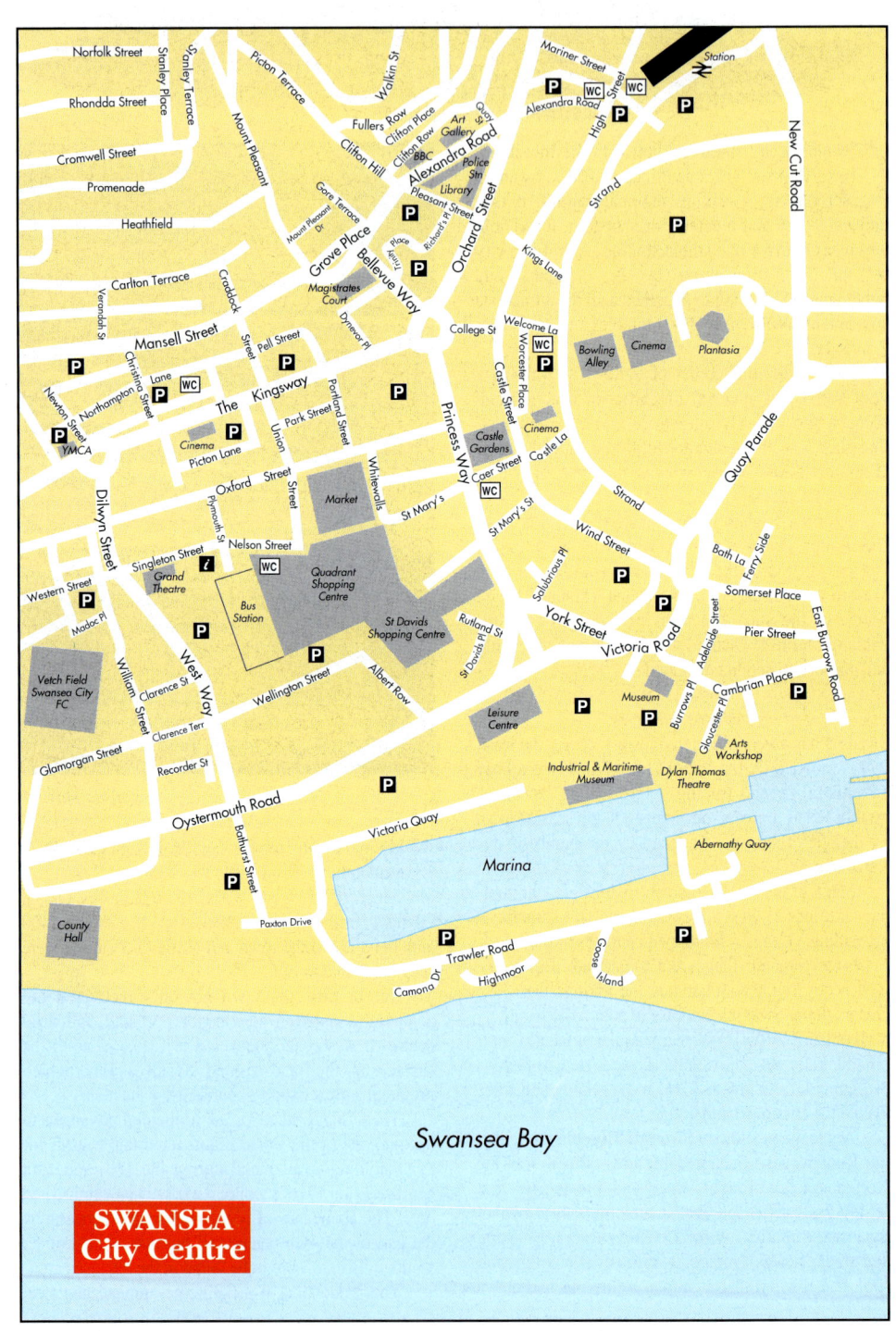

*The Premier Guide to Swansea Bay & Gower*

**SWANSEA City Centre**

developed alongside the copper industry, and south-west Wales became a centre of tinplate manufacture. By the 1890's about 75% of Britain's tinplate mills were located within 20 miles of Swansea, many of them in the Lower Swansea Valley.

This proliferation of heavy industry and collieries certainly created wealth, but it also destroyed much of the landscape of the valley. In 1960 work began in earnest on restoring it to something like its original state, and nearly 40 years later the Lower Swansea Valley is regarded as an excellent example of how land devastated by industrial activity and pollution *can* be reclaimed given time, effort, money and care.

Ironically, while industry was doing its worst for the environment of Swansea Bay in the 19th century, the area to the south and west of the town aspired to become a fashionable and stylish resort.

For a time it succeeded and was frequented by ladies and gentlemen to whom the continent was out of bounds because of the territorial ambitions of a certain Napoleon Bonaparte. The attentions of high society meant that by the early 1800's Swansea town centre boasted a reputable theatre, respectable hotels, bathing facilities, and a busy programme of balls, regattas, race meetings and cricket matches. And wealthy local industrialists, such as the Vivian family, built splendid homes to the west of the town.

However, it was Swansea's success as an industrial and maritime centre that went from strength to strength, peaking in the years that led up to the First World War but declining in the decades which followed as the metal industries slumped. The once-thriving docks were suddenly dependent solely on the export of anthracite and the import of oil for the refinery at nearby Llandarcy.

Swansea was dealt a further blow in February 1941 when the medieval and Victorian heart of the old town was torn out by air raids which destroyed many fine buildings, including St. Mary's church and the market. Rebuilding was a slow process, hindered by the continuing decline of the old industries.

But once again time proved to be a great healer. The steel industry was modernised, the economy began to improve and Swansea became a city and the administrative centre of West Glamorgan.

### Swansea today

In modern-day Swansea the emphasis is firmly on tourism and leisure, backed by a strong industrial and commercial presence. Shipping also makes a valuable

---

### A warm welcome awaits you at the Hilton National Swansea.

The hotel has 118 bedrooms all ensuite, colour TV and video channels, direct dial telephone, trouser press and tea & coffee making facilities. Our Leisure Centre offers the perfect place to relax. There is a swimming pool, well equipped gymnasium, sauna and sunbed.

Venturers Restaurant features a choice of popular dishes from around the world including Welsh specialities. In addition we feature a stunning selection of cold hors d'ouevres and hot carvery with prime roast joints carved by our chefs. Venturers Bar provides the ideal place to enjoy a pre-dinner aperitif or simply relax after the days sightseeing.

Ideally situated for numerous attractions in the Swansea Bay & Gower areas.

**HILTON**
NATIONAL
SWANSEA

Phoenix Way, Enterprise Park, Swansea SA7 9EG
Telephone: 01792 310330
Fax: 01792 797535

contribution to the local economy, one of the most regular visitors to the port being the daily Swansea-Cork passenger and car ferry.

This thriving and agreeable city by the sea is an ideal base from which to explore the areas to the east, north and west of Swansea Bay. But before that, it has many attractions and places of interest of its own to show you.

### Swansea Maritime Quarter & Marina

The award-winning Maritime Quarter is one of Swansea's most popular attractions. It is a very impressive redevelopment of the old South Dock, which from its opening in 1859 was instrumental in Swansea's expansion as a major exporter of coal and copper. Now, in place of the warehouses, coal hoists and railway embankments, you will find an attractive waterfront village with a host of interesting features – shops, pubs, eating places, the Dylan Thomas Theatre, craft workshops, floating exhibits, Swansea Leisure Centre, Industrial and Maritime Museum, nightclub and more – all clustered around the 600-berth marina, just a few minutes' walk from the city centre.

In 1993 the marina was greatly enhanced and extended with the building of the £17 million River Tawe Barrage – the first tidal river barrage (as opposed to flood defence system) to be completed anywhere in Britain. This structure stretches 70 yards (64 metres) across the mouth of the river so that the marina is accessible to boats at virtually all stages of the tide. Another benefit of the barrage's ingenious design is production of electricity by the built-in hydro-generator, which works with the changing tides. The barrage is also good for the environment. It prevents any sea pollution from entering the Tawe and has enhanced the appearance of the riverside at low tide.

### Dylan Thomas Theatre

For details of performances ring 01792 473238.

### Maritime and Industrial Museum

This novel museum is designed to entertain the whole family as well as to provide information about Swansea's past. It incorporates a working woollen mill and historic floating exhibits, such as an ex-Gower lightship. A tramshed display tells the story of the Mumbles Railway – the world's first passenger railway. For more information ring 01792 650351.

### The Marina Tower Observatory

Run by the Swansea Astronomical Society, the observatory houses Wales' largest telescope. Open in

---

**FEATURING**
*Panache*
RESTAURANT &
**The Grill Room**
SWANSEA'S OLDEST WINEBAR & RESTAURANT

**NO SIGN BAR LTD.**
56 Wind Street
Swansea SA1 1EG
**01792 655332**

ALL A LA CARTE MEALS ½ PRICE
including a wide selection of Vegetarian Meals
**MONDAY TO WEDNESDAY**
**7.00pm - 10.30pm**
Also a wide selection of home cooked bar meals from £1.75 - £4.80
Or enjoy a bottle of wine with a choice from our delicious Tapas Menu £1.50 - £3.00

**Call now to book**
**Freephone: 0500 456 760**

---

## Local Bus Services in Swansea and Gower

★ Buses to popular destinations
★ Summer Open Top service to Mumbles
★ Ride all day in Swansea with a Multiride ticket

For details & times call Swansea 580580

**SWT** *We're with you all the way!*

---

## NUMBER ONE *Wind Street*

1 Wind Street, Swansea SA1 1DE · Tel: 01792 456996

We specialise in French Provincial Cuisine and Local Fish & Seafood

**Menu Changes Daily**

| SET LUNCH ~ | Three Courses | £11.95 |
| | Two Courses | £9.50 |
| OPEN ~ | Monday to Saturday, | 12 ~ 2.30pm |
| | Wednesday to Saturday, | 7 ~ 9.30pm |

Egon Ronay and Good Food Guide Recommended
Chef/Patron Kate Taylor

summer months (daily times vary) and for winter "Star Parties". For more information ring 01792 873334.

### Swansea Arts Workshop Gallery
Located in the Maritime Quarter, this unique artist-run gallery has an exhibition gallery focusing on contemporary art and craft from Wales, Britain and abroad. For more information ring 01792 652016.

### Plantasia
Located on the Parc Tawe complex close to the Maritime Quarter, this huge glass pyramid contains over 5000 plants, as well as lizards, snakes, insects, an aviary and an aquarium. Its hothouse garden has 3 climatic zones, in which humidity, temperature, ventilation and light levels are computer-controlled. For more information ring 01792 474555.

### Swansea Shopping & Market
Although most of the old town was destroyed by air raids in 1941, Swansea's excellent modern shopping facilities reflect the fact that the area's population is approaching 200,000 and is massively swollen by visitors throughout the year.

A highlight not to be missed is the covered market. Swansea has been well known for its markets since medieval times, when they were held in the streets around the castle. A new market hall was built in the 1890's and was the pride of the town until it was badly damaged in 1941. The market is now located in the Quadrant Shopping Centre, yet still retains much of its old character and traditions. On offer is an excellent choice of fresh fish, seafood, local farm produce (ranging from Welsh lamb to vegetables), and specialities such as laverbread and Penclawdd cockles. The ruins of Swansea Castle stand near the city centre, one of eleven castles which bear testimony to Norman rule in the area.

### Swansea Museum
Established in 1841, this is the oldest museum in Wales and it occupies a classically-styled 19th-century building with an imposing colonnaded entrance. Items on display range from local archaeological finds to treasures from ancient Egypt. There are examples of 19th-century costume, Victorian collections of natural history, a collection of Swansea and Nantgarw porcelain and pottery, and a history trail of the Lower Swansea Valley. Admission to the museum is free. For further information ring 01792 653763.

### Glynn Vivian Art Gallery
Housed in an elegant Edwardian building in the city centre, this award-winning gallery contains examples of rare and richly-decorated Swansea Porcelain, as well as works by 19th-century maritime painters and distinguished local artist Ceri Richards. Also on show are European and Oriental ceramics, clocks and paperweights. Admission is free. For further information ring 01792 655006.

### Attic Gallery
One of Wales' leading privately-run galleries, which since 1962 has represented the work of established contemporary artists. For more information ring 01792 653387.

---

## GALLINI'S
*Whatever the occasion . . .
Gallini's provide the ideal setting.*
A wide choice of Italian and English Food with fresh fish from the trawlers!
• Fully Licensed Bar • Ample Parking
Opening Times: 12 noon - 3 pm Daily
6 pm - 12 midnight Tuesday to Saturday
**Pilots House Wharf, Swansea Marina
Telephone: 01792 456285**

---

• MUSICALS • OPERA •
## SWANSEA GRAND THEATRE
BALLET • COMEDY • DRAMA • PANTOMIME • DANCE • MUSIC

**For all your Top Live Entertainment in South West Wales**

**BOX OFFICE 01792 475715**

# THE LIGHT, BRIGHT HEART OF SWANSEA
## THE QUADRANT SHOPPING CENTRE
### YOUR FAVOURITE SHOPS – ALL UNDER ONE ROOF

The Quadrant Shopping Centre welcomes you to the very heart of the city of Swansea.

Enjoy a relaxing and comfortable day out at the Quadrant, all your favourite stores under one roof.

**OPEN MONDAY TO SATURDAY 9am - 6pm (Wednesday until 8pm)
Open Sundays for Christmas**

# SHOPPING IN SWANSEA

## "The ideal place to start your shopping tour."

**SHOPPING in Swansea** is a delight with so many top stores within short walking distance of each other.

The familiar facades found in every good shopping city are here, with plenty of traditional smaller retailers nestling beside them, all offering a quality of service so well known in Wales.

Set amidst pedestrianised shopping streets, the Quadrant Shopping Centre, with the adjoining bustling indoor market which dates back hundreds of years, is the ideal place to start your tour of city shops.

Whatever the weather, the Quadrant welcomes you to spacious malls under a clear glass roof. Enjoy a relaxing and comfortable day out, with 38 quality stores ready to cater for all needs and pockets, and coffee-shops and restaurants offering ease and refreshment if you need a break from browsing.

Adjoining bus station and multi-storey car park make the Quadrant easy to get to for the best day out in town.

# CITY AND COUNTY OF SWANSEA
## DINAS A SIR ABERTAWE

# SWANSEA MARKET

*Wales' premier retail market offering you a unique shopping experience*

*Unrivalled variety all under one roof and right in the heart of the City Centre*

Over 100 separate stalls plus areas allocated to "casual" traders for the sale of local and specialised produce such as Gower grown vegetables, cockles, laverbread etc.

*Local Specialities – You must try cockles and laverbread at Swansea Market, the largest covered market in Wales*

## SWANSEA MARINA

- Situated in the heart of the restored historic Maritime Quarter
- *Swansea Marina* has berths for 360 boats
- Excellent facilities include 24 hour security
- Bordered on one side by a sandy beach
- Town centre is within easy walking distance with shops, restaurants, cinemas and theatre
- Small boat rate £725 p.a. inclusive

**Lockside, Maritime Quarter, Swansea SA1 1WG**
**Tel: 01792 470310 Fax: 01792 463948**

### Grand Theatre

This is the number one venue for entertainment in south-west Wales, offering an all-year-round programme of variety – drama, ballet, opera, musicals, one-night shows and the top names in television. The restaurant and bar facilities also help to make a night out at the Grand a really special occasion, serving pre-show meals, special meal packages to complement the entertainment, and interval drinks. The Grand has three supervised car parks and is very easy to get to via junction 42, 45 or 47 of the M4. The Quadrant bus terminus is adjacent to the rear of the theatre and Swansea's High Street railway station is just a mile from the Grand. For further information and bookings (Visa and Access accepted) ring 01792 475715 between 9.30am and 8pm Monday to Saturday.

### Brangwyn Hall

This is the city's principal concert hall, offering performances by the world's finest orchestras, soloists and conductors. It is located within Swansea Guildhall and is named after the Brangwyn Panels – a stunning series of murals, based on the theme of the British Empire, painted by Sir Frank Brangwyn in the 1920's and 1930's, originally for the House of Lords. For more information ring 01792 302489.

### Taliesin Arts Centre

The Centre stages a varied programme of theatre, music, dance, film and the visual arts. For more information ring 01792 295438.

### St. Mary's Church

The medieval church of Swansea, founded in the 12th century, St. Mary's was badly damaged by bombs in the Second World War and rebuilt for the third time in 1955. The previous two occasions were in 1745 and 1898.

### Heyokah Centre Vegetarian Restaurant

The restaurant originated as a tearoom and offers a wonderful variety of teas, coffees, herb tisanes and spiced teas from around the world. Further refreshment comes in the form of wholistic therapies, a relaxing visit to the Flotation Room and participation in TAI CHIN, CHI KUNG and meditation classes. Books, candles, crystals, fragrant oils and other gifts are also available. For more information, including evening reservations, ring 01792 457880.

### The Fun House

Dedicated to children, the Fun House opens every day during school holidays. For more information ring 01792 585490.

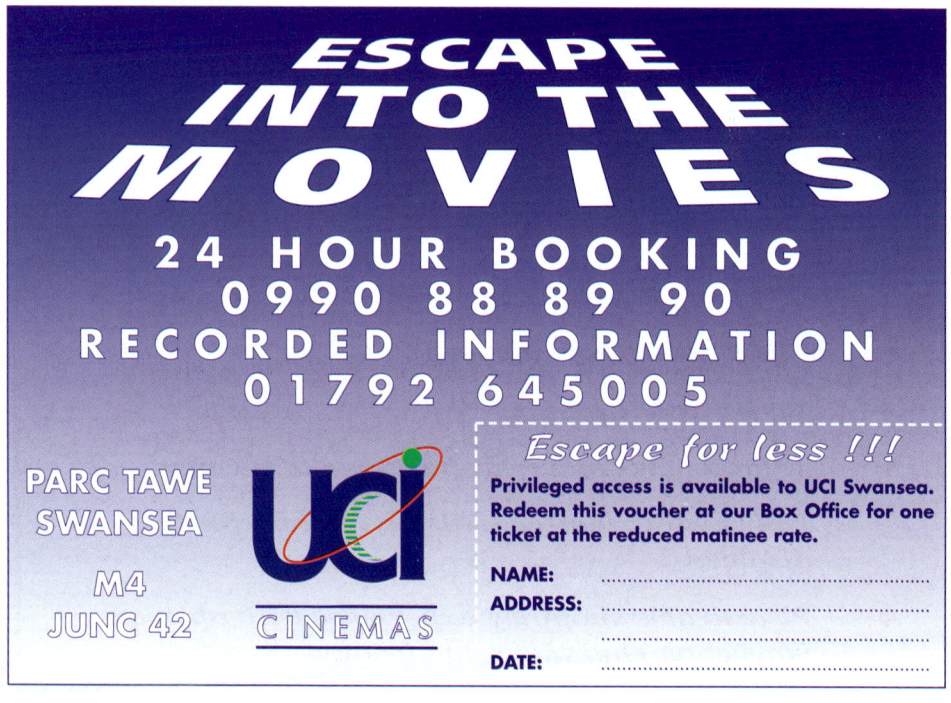

---

# ESCAPE INTO THE MOVIES

## 24 HOUR BOOKING
## 0990 88 89 90
## RECORDED INFORMATION
## 01792 645005

**PARC TAWE**
**SWANSEA**
**M4 JUNC 42**

**uci CINEMAS**

### Escape for less !!!

Privileged access is available to UCI Swansea. Redeem this voucher at our Box Office for one ticket at the reduced matinee rate.

NAME: ....................................................
ADDRESS: ...............................................
....................................................
DATE: ....................................................

# St Davids
## SHOPPING CENTRE
### SWANSEA

- ♦ **Easily accessible and central location**
- ♦ **Traffic free shopping**
- ♦ **Adjacent 560 space car park and taxi rank**
- ♦ **Fully pedestrianised with easy access for the disabled**
- ♦ **Pleasurable shopping experience with open air market on Thursdays and Fridays**

## Parks & Gardens

Nobody can accuse Swansea of lacking green fingers. In 1995 the city's parks won major trophies at the Royal Horticultural Society's rhododendron shows and three awards at the top Welsh horticultural shows. Not content to rest on their laurels, the city's parks staff, aided by community groups, also planted 1,500 trees, 20,000 saplings and countless thousands of bulbs.

The Swansea area enjoys an interesting variety of parkland – from the strict Victorian formality of Victoria Park, home of the bowls festival, to the natural rolling landscape of areas such as Morriston and Singleton and the many parks serving local communities. Singleton, close to the sea and university, is the venue for major summer events, including the vintage car rally and the horse and flower show which take place over the August bank holiday weekend. The Botanic Garden, sheltered by high walls, is open all year round, free of charge, and Singleton also has a boating lake, crazy golf course, extensive children's play area, cafe, and even its own pub!

A step away from Singleton is the area's oldest park, Brynmill. Loved by many locals, the park is a welcome oasis in a built-up area, its attractions including a fishing lake, small zoo, bowling green and a cafe.

The park most associated with Dylan Thomas is Cwmdonkin, which has a sunny sloping site and fine floral displays. Dylan was born at 5 Cwmdonkin Drive, a semi in the Uplands district of Swansea, in 1914. As a boy this park was one of his favourite haunts, and the memory of it merited several mentions in his poetry and prose. The park fondly remembers Dylan too, in the form of a memorial stone inscribed with lines from *Fern Hill,* one of his best-known and best-loved poems.

Clyne Gardens, once the private estate of the Vivian family, are supreme for their spring-flowering bulbs. Rhododendrons and azaleas from all over the world thrive here, as do unusual botanical specimens. Along with the botanical gardens in Singleton Park, Clyne forms a showcase for plants displayed under the National Collection Scheme.

Adjacent to Clyne Gardens, and only three miles west of the city centre, is Clyne Valley Country Park – one of four country parks in the Swansea area. Each exemplifies the subtle art of blending visitor facilities with natural attractions, and provides opportunities for cycling, riding and walking in an environment

---

## GOOD FOOD   GOOD WINE

### La BRASERIA

**28 WIND STREET • SWANSEA**
**TEL: 01792 469683**

Open Monday ~ Saturday 12 noon to 2.30pm
and 7.00pm to 11.30pm

**PRIVATELY OWNED,
PROFESSIONALLY RUN**

*The Restaurant with the difference.*
Enjoy the warm ambience & informality of
an authentic Spanish Bodega.
Where fresh food is complimented by an
extensive selection of wines and champagnes
to cater for all palates.
In addition to our A La Carte menu, whether
it's business or leisure, lunch should be a
pleasure, from our £6 for two courses menu.

# SWANSEA LEISURE CENTRE

## Your 1996 Summer Recipe for Family Fun & Fitness

### Ingredients

- 1 Ice Rink
- 1 Leisure Pool
- 250,000 Gallons of Water
- 1 Hydroslide
- 1 Blackhole
- 1 Jolly Roger
- 1 Fun Club

For further details please

☎ (01792) 649126

**SWANSEA LEISURE CENTRE**

*Your essential ingredient for family fun & fitness this summer*

**OYSTERMOUTH ROAD, SWANSEA**

CITY AND COUNTY OF SWANSEA
DINAS A SIR ABERTAWE

## Your instructions for a fun packed Summer!

Take 1 **Ice Rink** and leave to cool for the summer holiday. Flavour with ice-discos and special family-ice sessions.

• • •

Then take **250,000 gallons of water**. Heat gently to 84 degrees Fahrenheit (29 degrees Centigrade).

• • •

Add a **hydroslide**, a **blackhole**, **water chutes** and **kids interactive play area**. Mix well and serve with **waves** on a **beach** for at least 45 minutes.

• • •

For desert, try bouncy castles, ball ponds and soft play at the **Jolly Roger** and serve to children up to 7 years of age between 10am and 6pm during the school holidays and at weekends.

• • •

To round off, try a serving of the **Fun Club** for 5 to 13 year olds on Saturday, Monday, Tuesday and Thursday mornings between 9.30am to 12.30pm. Season with team games, arts and crafts, racket sports and swimming.

• • •

**Chef's Tip**: To accompany your visit, sample the refreshments in the Poolside Cafe or the Three Cliffs Bar.

… *Swansea Bay & Mumbles*

# the heyokah centre
## FOR HEALING ARTS & CRAFTS

## Vegetarian Café Restaurant

The Heyokah Centre Vegetarian Restaurant offers elegant dining in natural surroundings. Appetising wholefood cuisine prepared with organic produce from local sources. Enjoy Afternoon Tea beside the Amethyst Waterfall choosing from our selection of over one hundred teas and freshly baked cakes.

Candlelight and the open fire help to create an intimate setting for evening enjoyment. Vegan and macrobiotic choices are always available on our menus.

The Heyokah Centre Vegetarian Restaurant originated as a Tea Room within the Centre and consequently offers a wonderful variety of unusual teas, coffees, herb tisanes and spiced teas from all over the world.

To further refresh the weary, a wide range of wholistic therapies are available through the centre.

A visit to our Floatation Room provides relaxation in an especially tranquil environment both for those on holiday and local residents.

Visitors are welcome to join in ongoing TAI CHI, CHI KUNG, and Meditation classes in the Studio.

While wandering through the shop you will find beautiful books, candles, crystals and fragrant oils to enhance holiday hours or lovely gifts of stained glass, Native Crafts, jewellery and cards for those at home.

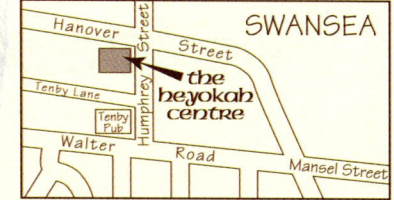

Opening hours - Monday through Saturday - 11.00 am - 5.30 pm
Evening Bookings - Thursday, Friday, Saturday from 6.00 pm
Telephone (01792) 457880 for reservations

2 Humphrey Street, Swansea SA1 6BG

# Taliesin Arts Centre
# University of Wales Swansea
# Singleton Park
# Swansea SA2 8PZ

## Box Office: (01792) 296883
## Administration: (01792) 295438

Taliesin Arts Centre is situated in the heart of the University campus, and is the only professional arts centre in the region. The purpose built arts centre is owned and run by the University and its exciting and wide-ranging activities are open to everybody.

Throughout the year there is a mixed programme of professional events, including the very best in theatre, dance, music, film and the visual arts. In recent years the centre has concentrated on extending its programme and has brought some of the finest national and international companies to Swansea. The centre has been recognised for its excellent film programming and has been awarded the status of Regional Film Theatre, by the British Film Institute.

The Ceri Richards Gallery operates on a self-financing commercial basis, and as well as staging regular exhibitions by some of Wales' finest artists, it also promotes the high quality work of artists from other countries. The retail outlet within the Gallery has also established itself as *the* venue for selling artists and craftspeoples work.

If you would like to find out more and would like a copy of Taliesin's **free** seasonal brochure, simply telephone the Box Office staff and they will be happy to forward one on to you.

*Swansea Bay & Mumbles*

# FORTE Posthouse

Kingsway Circle
Swansea
West Glamorgan SA1 5LS
Telephone: 01792 651074
Facsimile: 01792 456044

This modern, recently refurbished Forte Posthouse is within walking distance of Swansea's attractively developed marina and makes a handy base for trips to the beautiful Gower Peninsula.

- 99 bedrooms
- Lounge
- **Leisure Club** with heated indoor pool, fully equipped gym, sauna, solarium & beauty therapist
- Free, small car park
- **Family:** Baby listening, babysitting - notice required
- Informal restaurant & bar
- Room service
- Minibar, hairdryer & trouser press

## SILVERLINE

Quality Small Coaches Serving the Brecon Beacons

### Tel: 01874 623900
3 BEACONS VIEW, MOUNT ST, BRECON

**SILVERLINE** operates coach services every day from Brecon to Merthyr Tydfil, Neath and Swansea. At Merthyr Tydfil the coach connects with the Sprinter train to and from Cardiff. (And waits if the train is late) Through day tickets available from Brecon to Cardiff, Barry, Penarth, etc. giving reductions on entry to Techniquest, Rhondda Heritage Park and leisure centres at Barry, Merthyr Tydfil & Penarth.

## SWANSEA Tennis Centre

### Play *the* Game!

Kid's on court
Summer LEAGUE
Junior club

for details contact ...

Swansea Tennis Centre
Upper Bank, Landore,
Swansea SA1 7DS
☎ **(01792) 650484**

- Pay'N'Play
- Courses & Programmes
- Adult & Junior Sessions
- Mixed Up Doubles
- Little Smashers
- Short Tennis
- Transitional Tennis

CITY AND COUNTY OF SWANSEA
DINAS A SIR ABERTAWE

abundant with trees and plants. A new country park – the Loughor Riverside Park – is now being established on reclaimed land formerly occupied by the Broadoak Colliery.

The area's parks contain many fine historic buildings, such as those of the Singleton Park estate and the castles at Oystermouth and at Parc William in Loughor. The day-to-day running of Oystermouth is managed by a group of volunteers, The Friends of Oystermouth Castle, who have assisted in preparing a ten-year programme of improvements to make the castle one of the best historic sites in Wales.

The city's parks staff too have been carrying out environmental improvements as part of the policy of 'Greening the City'. This includes play and sports facilities in parks and other sites throughout the city and area.

### The Environment Centre

Open throughout the year (daily times vary), the Centre provides information on environmental organisations such as the National Trust and British Trust for Conservation Volunteers. For more details ring 01792 480200.

### Crymlyn Bog National Nature Reserve

The reserve is located at Bonymaen, just a mile north-east of Swansea city centre, and it affords a rare opportunity to view a wealth of plants, insects and birds in an unspoilt environment. The Visitor Centre has photographic displays of the species found here, and an illustrated history. An easy circular route has been established to take you along the edge of the bog, and other areas are accessible only with the warden's permission. The bog is managed by the Countryside Council for Wales and has free parking and a picnic area. Groups are welcome but it is essential to contact the warden first. For more information ring 01792 459255.

## Mumbles

From its eastern end, the long shoreline of Swansea Bay is broken by the River Tawe before curving round in a wide five-mile sweep to its southern tip at the Mumbles.

This village resort was discovered by the Victorians and has been a popular holiday destination ever since. It has everything you expect of a typical British seaside resort. A Victorian pier (900 feet long) with its fishermen, funfair, helter skelter, amusement arcade, cafe and nightclub; a wide expanse of sand and deckchairs; a long promenade, which extends back along the bay to the east of Swansea city centre; a lighthouse, built in 1793 and Mumbles' best-known landmark; an abundance of pubs, clubs and restaurants, scattered along the famous Mumbles Mile; and an assortment of gift and other shops where you can idly browse in the evening after a hard day of holiday enjoyment.

The Mumbles even has a castle, grander than Swansea's and perched on a hill above the village of Oystermouth. It is a development of the original Oystermouth Castle, which was destroyed by the Welsh in the 13th century, and is in a remarkably good state of preservation. From this lofty position the views over the bay and Mumbles Head are spectacular.

Oystermouth is in fact a more accurate name for the settlement which has come to be known as Mumbles, for this is the village around which the resort has grown up. The name is also a reflection of the once-thriving trade in local oysters. These days Oystermouth is a charming village of attractive streets lined with gift and craft shops, one of which has achieved considerable fame by specialising in traditional Welsh wooden lovespoons.

*Mumbles Head*

## TREASURE

A visit to Mumbles and Gower is not complete unless you call at

**TREASURE**
in Mumbles
A store full of unusual and exciting gifts for all the family

Join us for Morning Coffee, Lunch Time Bites, or Afternoon Teas in our Self Serve Restaurant, famous for its "home cooked" foods.

You'll enjoy your visit to **TREASURE** and make plans to come again.

**TREASURE**
29 - 33 Newton Road, Mumbles
Tel: 01792 361345

---

## Kate & Steve welcome you to P.A.'s Wine Bar

For people who appreciate good quality and the finer pleasures in life, P.A.'s offers excellent a la carte cuisine cooked to perfection by our expert chefs

Quality wines from around the World
Come and sample what everyone is talking about

95 Newton Road, Mumbles,
Swansea SA3 4BN
Tel: 01792 367723

---

## PARTIZAN

WHOLESALERS OF FAR FETCHED CLOTHES AND JEWELLERY

18 NEWTON ROAD, MUMBLES, SWANSEA
TEL: 01792 363147

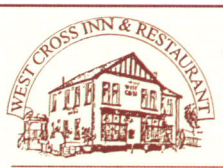

---

## WEST CROSS INN & RESTAURANT

43 MUMBLES ROAD, WEST CROSS, SWANSEA
TEL: (01792) 401143

**LUNCHTIMES & EVENING MEALS**
*Bar · Restaurant · Function Room*
*Beer Garden · Children Welcome*

**Proprietors:**
Len & Lavinia Morgans

---

## Families Welcome

Sample the new delicious additions to our menu, with family and friends in a friendly and party atmosphere at

**CJ's WINE BAR RESTAURANT**

135 Mumbles Road, Mumbles. Tel: 01792 361246

Fame is no stranger to Mumbles, having arrived here as early as 1804 with the opening of the Mumbles Railway to transport coal and limestone. It was horsedrawn and ran for about five miles from Swansea to Oystermouth. By 1807 it was also carrying up to eighteen passengers and so reputedly became the world's first ever passenger railway. In 1877 horse power was replaced by steam, and in 1929 there was further progression, this time to double-decker electric trams with a distinctive red livery.

The familiar sight of these trams found affection with locals and holidaymakers alike, and they were sorely missed when the service closed in 1960. One consolation, however, is that the journey can now be made along a cycle and pedestrian path which runs from Swansea Marina to Mumbles Pier. Bikes and tandems are readily available for hire.

Now a popular venue for water-skiing, windsurfing, yachting and other watersports, Mumbles is also the gateway to what was Britain's first officially-designated Area of Outstanding Natural Beauty – the Gower Peninsula.

### The Lovespoon Gallery
A unique gallery in Mumbles, dedicated entirely to Welsh lovespoons. For more information ring 01792 360132.

### PineNeedles Crafts
This tiny but charming shop at 14 Newton Road, Mumbles has an enticing range of Welsh crafts and handmade chocolates to aromatherapy oils and the ever-popular dragon in all its guises. The proprietors, the Jones family, produce their own unique gifts too, and items can be custom-made for you to take home. For more information ring 01792 363011.

### Oystermouth Castle
Enjoying panoramic views over Swansea Bay and Mumbles, the substantial remains of 13th-century Oystermouth Castle are in exceptionally good condition. It was built by the de Breos family, who ruled Gower until the 1320's, and it replaced the original 12th-century castle which had been destroyed by the Welsh. Designed more as a mansion than a fortress, it has many interesting features, including an elegant chapel window in the south-east tower. The castle is open to visitors during summer and plays host to open-air performances of opera and Shakespeare. For more information ring 01792 302411.

---

# Patricks

**638 Mumbles Road**
**Southend · Mumbles**

*Patricks* is a family run business that has been trading for two years with the philosophy of good value for money by serving seriously good food and drink from
Morning Coffee
Lunch Time Specials
Afternoon Tea
Dinner
through to Sunday Lunch

To book a table just telephone 01792 360199

**Contact us on 01792 360199**

### A Typical Daily Menu Includes:~
Home-made soup of the day
Warm mackerel fillet with a horseradish potato salad
Thai spiced chicken pieces & prawns garnished with prawn crackers
Mulled poached pears with walnuts & crumbled stilton
~
Chicken breast on field mushrooms with a garlic spinach sauce
Lamb shank studded with garlic & rosemary on a red wine sauce
Salmon with a cheese & prawn crust on a fresh tomato sauce
Fresh flour tortillas loaded with Mexican spiced vegetables with a duo of yogurt & tomato salsa
~
Simply fruit
Crispy macaroons with coconut ice-cream & a sticky caramel sauce
Old fashioned treacle tart & custard
Duo of chocolate tort with raspberry coulie

*All main course dishes are served with fresh vegetables or mixed salad*

# SWANSEA
## OUTDOOR LEISURE

As one of Wales' premier holiday resorts, Swansea combines the facilities of a bustling port and maritime city with some of the finest beaches, rural beauty, and Outdoor Leisure Attractions to be found anywhere in Britain.

If you are in the area this summer, don't miss out on the following outdoor activities!

- play **Tennis** at beautiful Langland Bay
- try **Putting** and **Crazy Golf** at Mumbles Gardens
- superb **Bowling Greens** are available at Mumbles, Victoria and Cwmdonkin Park - with equipment available at no extra charge
- for a sterner test, look no further than the **9 Hole Pitch & Putt Course** at Blackpill Burrows, which runs behind Swansea Bay
- visit **Singleton Boating Lake**, one of Swansea's most popular visitor attractions, with its fantastic free children's play area, rowing boats, and pedaloes for hire, crazy golf and bouncy castles.

**For further information telephone**
**SWANSEA (01792) 636000**

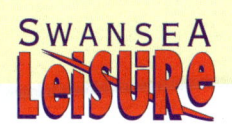

SWANSEA
Leisure

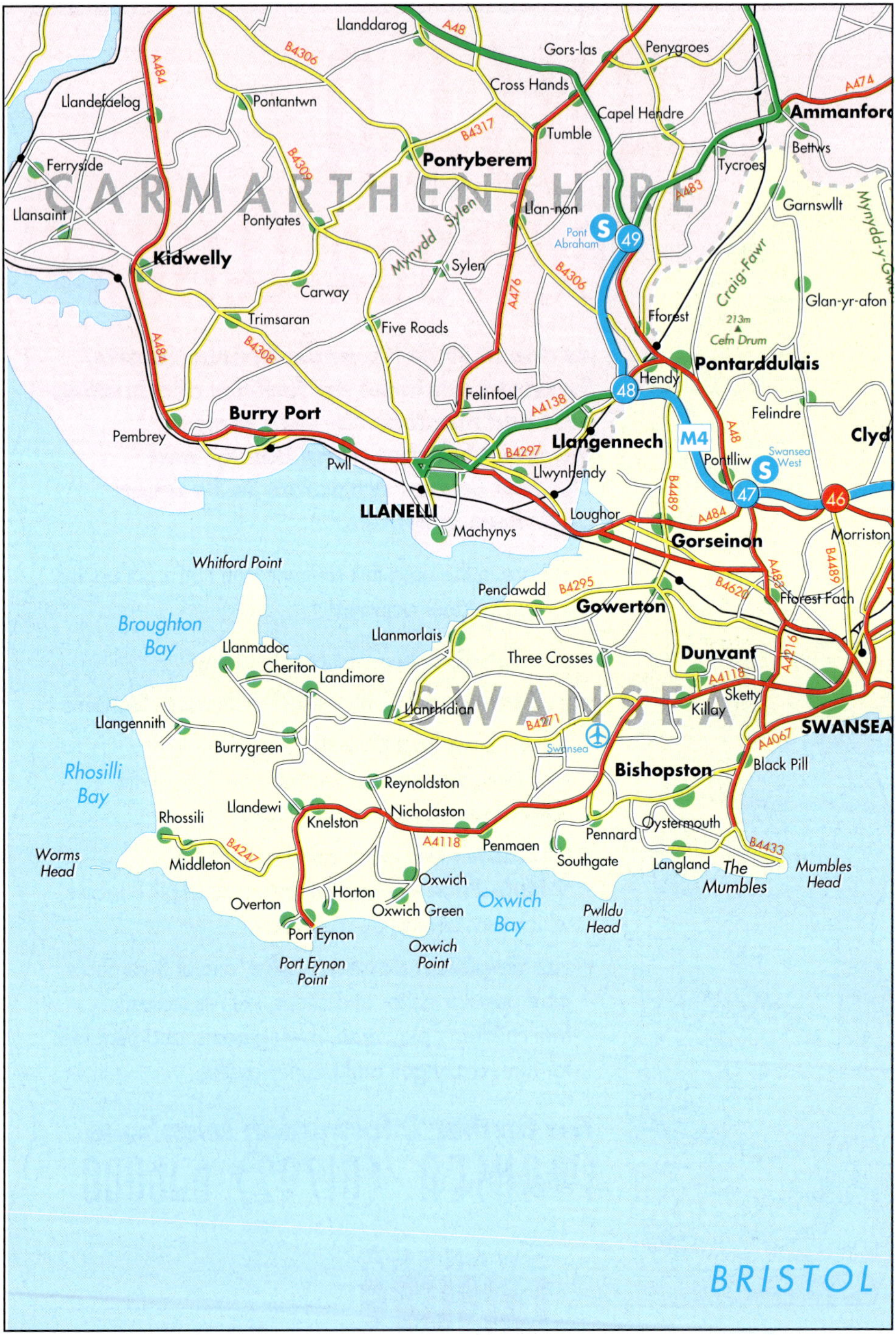
Llanddarog
A48
B4306
Gors-las
Penygroes
A484
Cross Hands
A474
Llandefaelog
Pontantwn
Capel Hendre
Ammanford
B4317
Tumble
Ferryside
Pontyberem
Bettws
B4309
Tycroes
CARMARTHENSHIRE
A483
Llansaint
Llan-non
Garnswllt
Pontyates
Mynydd Sylen
Pont Abraham
S
49
Mynydd-y-Gw
Kidwelly
Sylen
B4306
Craig-Fawr
Carway
A476
Glan-yr-afon
Trimsaran
Fforest
213m
Cefn Drum
Five Roads
A484
B4308
Pontarddulais
Hendy
48
Felinfoel
A4138
Felindre
Burry Port
M4
Clyd
Pembrey
A48
Llangennech
Swansea West
B4297
Pontlliw
S
Pwll
Llwynhendy
B4489
47
46
LLANELLI
Loughor
A484
Morriston
Machynys
Gorseinon
Whitford Point
B4489
A483
Penclawdd
B4295
B4620
Fforest Fach
Broughton Bay
Gowerton
Llanmorlais
Llanmadoc
Three Crosses
Dunvant
Cheriton
A4216
Landimore
A4118
Sketty
SWANSEA
Llanrhidian
Killay
Llangennith
B4271
SWANSEA
Swansea
A4067
Burrygreen
Black Pill
Rhosilli Bay
Reynoldston
Bishopston
Llandewi
Nicholaston
Rhossili
Knelston
Oystermouth
Pennard
A4118
Penmaen
B4247
B4433
Worms Head
Southgate
Middleton
Langland
The Mumbles
Mumbles Head
Oxwich
Horton
Oxwich Bay
Overton
Oxwich Green
Pwlldu Head
Port Eynon
Oxwich Point
Port Eynon Point
BRISTOL

37

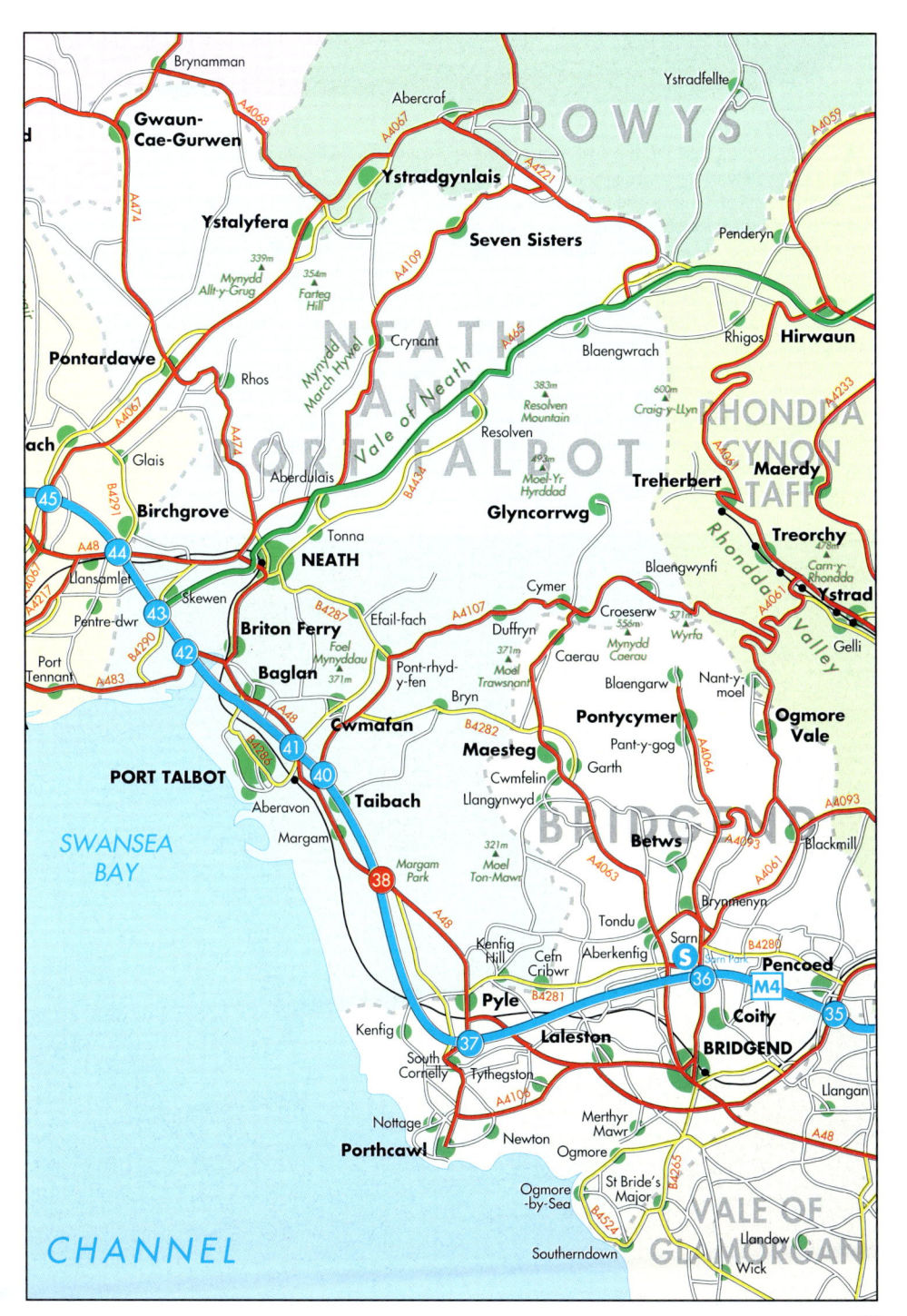

# The Gower Peninsula

Although joined at the hip to Swansea, the Gower Peninsula is virtually untouched by development – a world apart from the industrial and urban spread that characterises other parts of South Wales, and without a single town to its name.

Gower is remarkable in many respects. Designated Britain's first Area of Outstanding Natural Beauty, in 1956, the peninsula measures approximately 14 miles from east to west and about half that distance across. Within these narrow shores you can explore a great diversity of landscape: cliffs towering above golden beaches and rocky coves; hilltops commanding spectacular views over Welsh and English coastlines; and open downs and wide commons leading to vast areas of saltmarsh and sand dunes.

This gloriously unspoilt scene is further enhanced by deep wooded valleys and the ruins of medieval castles and ancient burial sites. There are attractions natural and man-made, and something new to discover at every turn. Yet even the peninsula's most westerly beach, Rhossili, is within easy driving distance of the shops and amenities of Swansea's bustling city centre.

One of the many striking features of Gower is the difference between the northern and southern coastlines. The north is a wild estuarine landscape of saltmarsh and mudflats, for the most part devoid of human activity. Yet in the south the picture is of

*Oxwich Church*

*Rhossili Bay*

*The Premier Guide to Swansea Bay & Gower*

## GOWER HOLIDAY VILLAGE

Tastefully set in spacious grounds, our comfortable two bedroomed bungalows provide a high standard of accommodation and are ideally located to enjoy the scenic beauty of Gower. Free heated indoor swimming pool with spa bath, Sauna, solarium, games room, putting green, playground, launderette, shop & hairdressers.

Scurlage, Nr Port Eynon, Swansea, S Gower SA3 1AY
**Tel: 01792 390431**

## The North Gower Hotel

16 En Suite Bedrooms
a la carte Restaurant (open evenings)
Bar Meals lunchtime & evenings

Set in its own mature landscaped gardens, overlooking the beautiful Loughor Estuary, and surrounded by some of the most breathtaking coastal and rural scenery on the Gower peninsula.

**COMMENDED**

Enquiries welcome
Llanrhidian, Gower, Swansea SA3 1EE
Telephone: 01792 390042

## King Arthur Hotel
### A Superb Gower Country Inn

Delightfully refurbished accommodation. All bedrooms (two with four-poster beds) are en suite. Children welcome. B&B from £25 single, £45 double. Featured in *The Good Weekend Guide*.

Extensive bar and restaurant menu. Our home-cooked fare includes local produce. Featured in *The Good Pub Guide*.

A great traditional village inn atmosphere, with log fires, folk evenings etc, and a fine range of real ales. Featured in C.A.M.R.A's *The Good Beer Guide*.

We also have a beer garden, children's playground and a large car park.

Reynoldston · Gower · Swansea SA3 1AD
Tel: 01792 391099 or 01792 390775

## Unique Setting by the Sea

### OXWICH BAY HOTEL

Oxwich Bay · Gower ·
Nr Swansea · SA3 1LS

☎ **01792 390329**

Ideal venue for exploring the Gower Peninsula.
OPEN ALL YEAR to residents and non-residents.

*Bargain Breaks* from £70.00 per person for two nights (Full Board Accommodation).

Colour Brochure sent with pleasure.

*Serving you with pleasure!*

magnificent sandy beaches, secluded bays and dramatic headlands – a holiday paradise for families, fishermen and watersports enthusiasts.

Separating north from south is the ridge of hills known as Cefn Bryn. The views from here are tremendous, looking one way over the Loughor estuary to Carmarthenshire and the other towards Three Cliffs Bay and the Bristol Channel. Ancient ancestors evidently appreciated this perspective too, for on Cefn Bryn stands the giant cromlech called Arthur's Stone – a Neolithic burial chamber which has a 25-ton capstone.

Inevitably, Gower's magnetic attraction can result in traffic congestion at the height of summer, while some of the more remote beaches are not accessible by road at any time. But this should not worry the true explorer, for the peninsula is best seen on foot, bike or horseback. You can walk almost the entire coastline, and an exhilarating cliff path runs from Mumbles along the south coast to Worms Head – just one of the many delights awaiting you in this beautifully unspoilt corner of South Wales.

## The North Coast

Gower's north coast is dominated by Llanrhidian Marsh – six miles of saltmarsh adjoining the mudflats and sandbanks of the Loughor estuary, and home to grazing sheep and wild ponies.

The marsh also attracts a great variety of birds. These include wildfowl, shellduck and huge numbers of waders such as oystercatchers, plovers and redshanks which flock here in winter months to feed on the rich pickings of the tidal mudflats.

The estuary is a designated Ramsar site, which means it is a protected wetland conservation area of international importance. This is not its only role. Some of the biggest cockle beds in Wales are to be found at Penclawdd, and for generations cockle gathering has been an important local industry on this part of Gower.

To the west of Llanrhidian Marsh lies the three-mile promontory of Whiteford Burrows and Whiteford Sands, where there is a National Nature Reserve. At the northern end of the sands is Whiteford Point.

Just off the point stands a disused cast-iron lighthouse which was built in 1865 and decommissioned in 1933. Its function is now performed by an automatic light on the island of Burry Holms, between the bays of Broughton and Rhossili, four miles to the south-west.

## The West Coast

Gower's west coast is blessed with one of the finest beaches in Britain – Rhossili. It is overlooked by Rhossili Down, which at 634 feet is the highest hill on the peninsula. Archaeologists have literally had a field day here, as many ritual and burial sites dating from the Bronze Age have been discovered around the top of the Down.

Near the crest there are also the remains of two ancient burial chambers known as Sweyne's Howes. By tradition these are associated with the Viking warlord Sweyne – allegedly the founder of the community which developed into the city of Swansea – but they are actually Neolithic, between 4,000 and 5,500 years old.

On a clear day Rhossili Down gives panoramic views over Gower and South Pembrokeshire, and across the Bristol Channel to Somerset, Devon and Lundy Island. The Down also provides one of

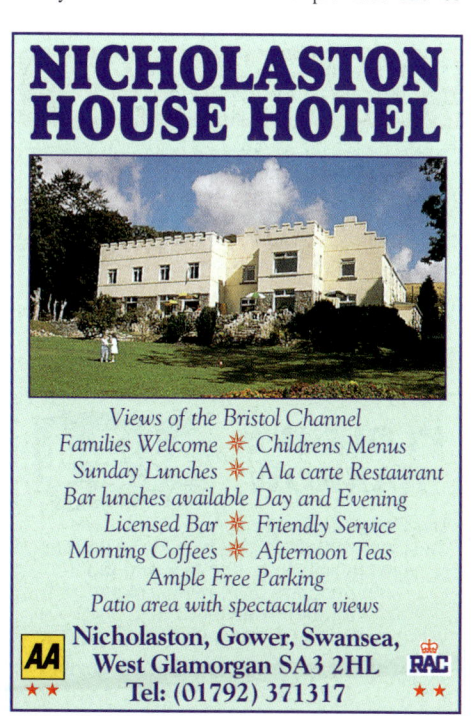

**NICHOLASTON HOUSE HOTEL**

Views of the Bristol Channel
Families Welcome ✻ Childrens Menus
Sunday Lunches ✻ A la carte Restaurant
Bar lunches available Day and Evening
Licensed Bar ✻ Friendly Service
Morning Coffees ✻ Afternoon Teas
Ample Free Parking
Patio area with spectacular views

AA  Nicholaston, Gower, Swansea,
West Glamorgan SA3 2HL  RAC
Tel: (01792) 371317

Gower's best walks, from Rhossili village to Hillend.

Below the Down is the magnificent sweep of Rhossili Bay – three miles of clean golden sand frequented by fishermen, surfers and hang gliders. Towards the southern end of this wonderful beach are the decaying remains of the barque *Helvetia*, which was blown ashore one night in November, 1887. Behind the beach are the dunes which hide the lost village of old Rhossili, a community engulfed by the sand. The church of the present-day village has a memorial to Edgar Evans, who died with Scott in the Antarctic in 1912.

At the southern tip of Rhossili Bay, the serpent-like peninsula of Worms Head extends west for a mile into the sea. For a short period either side of low tide you can walk across it, but there are restrictions on access during the bird-nesting season, as the site is the South Gower Coast National Nature Reserve, managed by the Countryside Council for Wales.

Rhossili also has another attraction – the National Trust Visitor Centre and shop, which is housed in two former coastguard cottages.

## The South Coast

The limestone cliffs of Gower's very popular south coast are punctured by caves in which remains of early man and animals have been discovered. The finds are proof that the mammoth, cave bear, reindeer and woolly rhinoceros have all used these caves for shelter in the distant past.

The best-known cave is Paviland, which is east of Thurba Head and famous for the so-called Red Lady of Paviland. This was a headless skeleton stained with red ochre, discovered in 1823 and thought to be that of a woman from the Roman period. Later tests and carbon dating proved it to be that of a young man who lived about 24,000 years ago. The skeleton is now in the University Museum, Oxford.

The most unusual cave is Culver Hole, near Port Eynon – a sea cave which poses a mystery still unsolved. The entrance of the cave has been almost entirely blocked by a strong masonry wall which rises to a height of four storeys, each marked by a "window"; the windows are connected on the inside by a flight of stone steps. The purpose of this bizarre structure is completely unknown, though the theories proposed have linked it variously with the lost castle of Port Eynon, a home for pigeons and a hideout for smugglers!

Another interesting cave is Minchin Hole, which is east of Three Cliffs Bay and south of the village of Southgate. It is the largest bone cave on Gower, and excavations have revealed hearths, cooking pots, bone spoons, combs, bronze brooches and spindle whorls, suggesting occupation during Iron Age and Roman periods. The animal bones found here include those of the woolly mammoth, woolly rhinoceros, narrow-nosed rhinoceros, elephant, lion and hyena.

East of Minchin Hole, just west of Pwll Du Head, is Bacon Hole. Rhinoceros and elephant bones

---

**Great Food ~ Great Atmosphere
You've Got To Try It!**

## SEASONS BISTRO
**INCORPORATING THE VILLAGE INN**

**1st Class Freshly Prepared
Continental and Traditional Cuisine**

Locally grown produce accompanied by
a very good selection of wines ~
and all at sensible prices!

**OPEN TUESDAY - SATURDAY**

**CALL (01792) 203311 FOR RESERVATIONS**
5 & 6 Swan Court, off Gower Road,
Killay, Swansea

---

## PITTON CROSS CARAVAN AND CAMPING PARK

Peaceful family park renowned for spectacular views to Lundy Island, Brecon Beacons. Flat site, good access, near to beaches, footpaths, Worms Head, National Trust Centre. From Swansea A4118 sign post South Gower to Scurlage B4247 to Rhossili, entrance 2 miles on left.

Open April - October

*Colour brochure a pleasure*

**Rhossili, Swansea SA3 1PL
Tel: (01792) 390593**

---

## PLOUGH & HARROW

The Plough & Harrow is one of the areas best known Inns. It provides for its patrons a warm welcome, fine ales and food.
Our country fayre menu offers a wide variety of dishes.
We hope you enjoy our pub and will visit us.

**Oldway Road, Murton, South Gower
Tel: 01792 234459**

*Llanrhidian*

have also been found in this cave, along with later mammals such as the wild ox, wolf and red deer.

However, it is the beaches of Gower's south coast which rank as its star attraction. They are sandy, unspoilt and almost totally uncommercialised, and some of the most secluded and appealing beaches are not very accessible, as described on pages 5-8.

Gower's beaches also offer great variety. For example, at the Mumbles (eastern) end of the south coast you will find the small but popular coves of Bracelet Bay and Limeslade Bay, while the bays of Rotherslade, Langland and Caswell are larger family beaches, also well patronised.

Further west, Three Cliffs Bay is one of the most picturesque on the Gower Peninsula, overlooked by the ruins of Pennard Castle and separated from the hugely popular Oxwich Bay by the headland of Great Tor.

Then there is pretty Port Eynon, with its whitewashed cottages, excellent facilities and large sandy beach. Before the arrival of tourists Port Eynon was busily engaged in oyster fishing, limestone quarrying, lobstering and crabbing. It also enjoyed notoriety for another activity – smuggling. So prevalent was smuggling along this coastline that at one time no fewer than eight excise men were stationed in this one small village!

The most westerly beach of Gower's south coast is Mewslade Bay. Secluded, isolated and sandy, it is set between Thurba Head and Tears Point, amongst magnificent cliff scenery.

### Guardians of Gower

Fortunately for all who appreciate its great natural beauty, Gower enjoys protection in many ways.

For example, ten per cent of the peninsula is owned and managed by the National Trust, who also own a large proportion of the coastline. Then there are official designations of sites recognised to be of environmental and landscape importance. These include three National Nature Reserves, a Local Nature Reserve, a Ramsar Site (wetland of international importance), more than a dozen Sites of Special Scientific Interest (SSSI), a Special Protection Area, and 34 miles of Heritage Coast.

Six of these protected sites are in the care of the Glamorgan Wildlife Trust, which was established in

*The Premier Guide to Swansea Bay & Gower*

Weobley Castle

1961. The Trust's emblem is the eider duck – chosen because the Burry Inlet is the only site in Wales where the eider resides all year round. The sites, covering 238 acres of Gower's south coast, stretch from Port Eynon to Rhossili and contain some of the most magnificent sea cliffs in Wales. They are also home to a great variety of birds, flowers and animals, along with smaller creatures of the seashore such as mussels and whelks.

For 1996 the Gower Countryside Service has compiled a programme of special events to mark the peninsula's 40th anniversary as an Area of Outstanding Natural Beauty – a status which in itself is enough to protect Gower from major development. Such a designation aims to achieve the very delicate balance between conserving the landscape and its wildlife yet encouraging people to enjoy the area without damaging it.

For more information about the Gower Countryside Service's programme of events, which range from guided walks to the pursuit of bats to a week's experience of drystone walling with the National Trust, ring 01792 302741.

---

Customers old and new are welcome to
## BWTHYN CRAFTS

*For selected crafts and gifts all made in Wales including*
Ceramics, Decorative Glass, Welsh Slate, Welsh and Jacob Wool, Hand Made Wooden Gifts, Jewellery, Local Interest Books and Maps, Preserves, Dressings, Boxed Confectionery (including Caldey Island Chocolate) and much much more at Bwthyn Crafts

Oxwich, Gower SA3 1LS · Tel (01792) 390686

---

## GOWER
**Beautiful Gower Peninsular**
### New Luxury Holiday Homes
for hire on 30 acre woodland caravan park.
**Open March to December**
Ideally situated for walks, golf, beaches and Swansea ~ Mumbles

**Blackhills Caravan Park, Blackhills Lane, Fairwood Common, Swansea SA2 7JN**
Tel: 01792 207065  Fax: 01792 280995

### Bishop's Wood Countryside Centre and Local Nature Reserve

Adjacent to Caswell Bay beach, the reserve is 46 acres of woodland and grassland. There are various short nature trails and also a small Visitor Centre. For more information ring 01792 361703.

### Black Hills Leisure, Fairwood Common

Set in a relaxing 30-acre woodland site only three miles from Three Cliffs Bay, this family-run business offers new static holiday home caravans for sale and rent. The site has a children's play area and licensed shop. For more information ring 01792 207065.

### Bwthyn Crafts, Oxwich

Welsh crafts, local-interest books and a very wide range of gifts are the attraction in this small but attractive shop – and everything on sale is made in Wales. For more information ring 01792 390686.

---

**GOWERTON**
GOLF RANGE & PAR 3 GOLF COURSE

- No membership required - families & beginners welcome
- 9-hole practice putting green and practice bunker
- Golf Shop and golf lessons
- Coffee Shop
- Ample safe car parking
- Open 8am until 1 hr before dusk

Visit us now at
VICTORIA RD, GOWERTON
(Nr Swansea Sound)

Tel: 01792 875188
Fax: 01792 874288

---

### Gowerton Golf Range

This 9-hole par 3 course and floodlit range is within easy reach of Swansea city centre and has 20 all-weather bays and 5 outdoor bays. The course features holes up to 164 yards long and is set in beautiful woodland, with bushes, ponds and the River Llan providing additional natural hazards. There is also a floodlit 9-hole putting green, golf shop, equipment hire, coffee shop and free parking.

*Port Eynon church*

No membership is required and families and beginners are welcome. For more information ring 01792 875188.

### Gower Surf Company
Specialising in wet suits at very competitive prices, this is the biggest surf shop in the area and is conveniently located for both north and south Gower. Open 7 days a week throughout the year, it also sells and hires out surfboards and body boards. Hire equipment is available only on production of a passport or credit card. For more information ring 01792 297276.

### National Trust Visitor Centre, Rhossili
The Centre is an ideal starting point from which to explore and enjoy this beautiful area. An exhibition illustrates Rhossili life and gives an insight into the National Trust's conservation work. For more information ring 01792 390636.

### Oxwich Castle
The remains of this fortified Tudor manor house overlook the bay and are open daily throughout the summer. For more information contact Cadw (Welsh Historic Monuments) on 01222 500200.

### PineNeedles Crafts, Parkmill
Located within the Gower Heritage Centre (Y Felin Ddwr), PineNeedles Crafts offers a wide range of made-in-Wales gifts, including unique items produced by the proprietors (the Jones family) themselves. The business also operates from a shop at 14 Newton Road, Mumbles. For more information ring 01792 232917 (Parkmill) or 363011 (Mumbles).

### Small World Pony Centre, Llanrhidian
This novel and interesting visitor attraction is the home of miniature ponies and other animals which represent the smallest of their breed, including sheep, pigs and pygmy goats. There is plenty here for families to see and do. For more information ring 01792 390995.

### The Salthouse, Port Eynon
Reputedly the haunt of smugglers, the Salthouse is associated with local pirate John Lucas. It is open throughout the year and admission is free. For more information ring 01792 302741 (Gower Countryside Services.)

### Weobley Castle
This was a fortified manor house rather than a full-blown Norman stronghold. It is perched above the Llanrhidian marshes, with beautiful views across the marshland and Loughor estuary. Built in the late 13th century, it suffered damage at the hands of Owain Glyndwr in 1406. It is now in the care of Cadw (Welsh Historic Monuments), and houses a local history exhibition. For more information ring 01792 390012.

### Y Felin Ddwr: Gower Heritage Centre
This 14th-century water mill and working craftshops, based around an old farm complex, is a rare example of how country skills and trades were often practised together in rural Wales. The waterwheel and corn-grinding machinery are intact and the Centre is open all year round, with parking, refreshments, a picnic area and access for disabled visitors. For more information ring 01792 371206.

---

## PineNeedles Crafts
You are welcome to visit our tiny shop where we have a lovely range of Welsh crafts and gifts.

*Bookends · Mirrors · Clocks · Letter Racks · Keyrings · Childrens Nameplaques and Name Jigsaws etc.*

**Also,** *Pembertons Victorian Handmade Chocolates (including chocolate lovespoons), Paintings, Prints, Pottery, Woodturning, Cards, Soft Toys, Aromatherapy Oils and Skincare.*

14 Newton Road · Mumbles · Tel: 01792 363011

---

## BANK FARM LEISURE PARK
Bank Farm, this a lovely 75 acre site, has breath-taking views of Horton and Port Eynon Bays.
Park Holiday Homes, Pitches for Touring Caravans and Tents are available. We have excellent amenities (including swimming pool, licensed bar and shop at the village entrance to the site), plus facilities for the disabled.
The new nautical lounge bar/function room opened in May 1992. There are many opportunities for coastal and rural leisure and sporting activities nearby.
With this much to offer, you are assured of a most memorable holiday - visit Bank Farm once and you'll want to return!
For Brochure and Booking form, write to Mr B Richards, Bank Farm, Horton, Gower, Swansea, SA3 1LL
Tel: (01792) 390228 Fax: (01792) 391842

**BANK FARM**

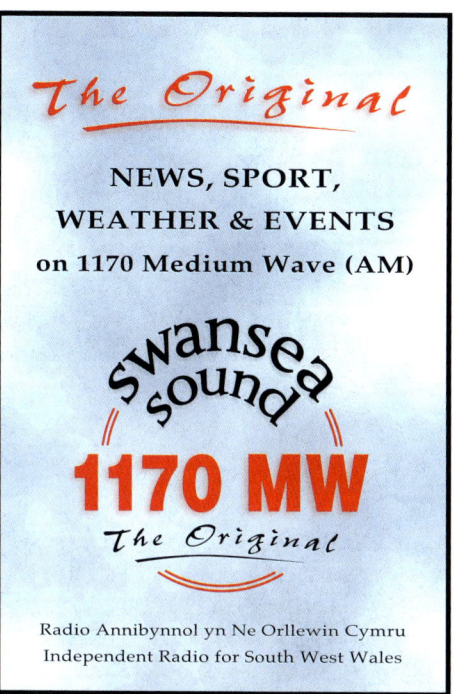

## The Original

**NEWS, SPORT, WEATHER & EVENTS**

on 1170 Medium Wave (AM)

*swansea sound*

**1170 MW**

*The Original*

Radio Annibynnol yn Ne Orllewin Cymru
Independent Radio for South West Wales

---

## SOUND WAVE 96.4 FM

**THE BIGGEST THING TO HIT YOUR RADIO IN 21 YEARS**

---

## Get the most from your visit to Swansea & Gower

Where to go!
What to do!
What to see!
Where to eat!
Where to shop!
Today and everyday

**South Wales Evening Post**

**FOR THE MOST...**

ADELAIDE STREET, SWANSEA.    TEL: (01792) 650841

# Neath Port Talbot...

*Aquadome*

*Cefn Coed Colliery Museum*

*Penscynor Wildlife Park*

*Aberavon Beach*

*Margam Park*

*Gunsmoke*

## ...surprisingly different

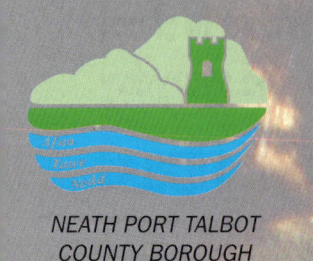

**For further information and for bed bookings in season contact: Pontneddfechan Tourist Information Centre on (01639) 721795 or Llandarcy Tourist Information Centre on (01792) 813030.**

NEATH PORT TALBOT COUNTY BOROUGH COUNCIL

# The Vale of Neath

The beautiful Vale of Neath today typifies the changing face of the South Wales valleys. The decline of the coal industry saw the last of the area's deep mines close in 1990, and coal tips and industrial dereliction have been swept away by the new broom of land reclamation. From the revitalised town of Neath itself to the upper reaches of the Nedd and Dulais rivers, the area is attracting a new generation of visitors in ever-growing numbers.

There is plenty for them to see. At its northern end, in the foothills of the Brecon Beacons National Park, the Vale of Neath is famous for the number and variety of its spectacular waterfalls – unique in Britain and much admired for more than two centuries by a succession of artists, poets, writers, photographers and film makers. Thomas Horner painted a series of watercolours of the Vale of Neath in 1819, but the most famous visiting artist was J.M.W. Turner, who painted Aberdulais Falls.

Neath was founded in the Middle Ages and now boasts an attractive new pedestrianised and landscaped town centre – the product of a £25 million urban regeneration scheme, which included restoration of a four-mile stretch of the Neath Canal. Behind the main shopping centre, housed in two Grade II listed buildings, is Neath Borough Museum, and overlooking the whole scene is all that remains of Neath Castle. Built in 1284 and the administrative

*Aberdulais Falls*

# NEATH Hotels & Guest Houses

### CWMBACH COTTAGES
Cwmbach Road,
Cadoxton,
Neath SA10 8AH
Tel: 01639 639825

HC

*In an idyllic setting, surrounded by woodlands, with panoramic views. Converted to high standard, all rooms en suite. Private car park and gardens.*

### GREEN LANTERNS GUEST HOUSE
Hawdref Ganol Farm,
Cimla, Neath SA12 9SL
Tel: 01639 631884

HC

*A warm welcome awaits you at our family run guest house, set in 45 acres nestling on a hillside. Panoramic views over the Vale of Neath just a mile from the birthplace of Richard Burton. West Glamorgan's only AA premier selected guest house (10 mins M4).*

### OAKTREE PARC
### HOTEL & RESTAURANT LTD
Birchgrove Road,
Birchgrove, Swansea SA7 9JR
Tel: 01792 817781
Fax: 01792 814542

C    AA & RAC 2 star

*Tastefully refurbished gentlemen's country residence, maintaining its original charm and family atmosphere, whilst offering all the amenities and comforts of a first class hotel, with superb A La Carte restaurant.*

### TREE TOPS GUEST HOUSE
282 Neath Road, Briton Ferry,
Neath SA11 2SL
Tel: 01639 812419

HC

*Tree Tops offers a warm welcome and good home cooking, rooms are tastefully furnished. Situated on the A474 at Briton Ferry 1.5 miles from Neath & 6 miles from Swansea. 1.5 miles from M4.*

### TY'N-Y-CAEAU
Margam Village,
Port Talbot SA13 2NW
Tel: 01639 883897

C

*17th Century vicarage in walled gardens. En suite large bedrooms with mountain and garden views. Close to Margam Abbey and park, Kenfig Nature Reserve and golf courses. Easy access off A48 dual carriageway near Jct 38 of M4 motorway. Always a warm Welsh welcome.*

### CONWAY GUEST HOUSE
30 Victoria Gardens,
Neath SA11 3BH
Tel: 01639 642364

*A small family run guest house situated in the centre of Neath near to the bus and railway stations, also a number of attractions. Colour TV and tea/coffee in all rooms.*

### GNOLL PARK MOTEL & RESTAURANT
77 Cimla Road,
Neath SA11 3TT
Tel: 01639 645656
Fax: 01639 646284

*A friendly family run motel where you can be assured of a warm welcome. There are 24 bedrooms all en suite with colour TV, direct line telephone, central heating and tea/coffee making facilities. Fully licensed bar and restaurant. Park outside your own motel door.*

centre of the town in the medieval period, the castle is currently under restoration.

The Vale of Neath's contribution to the industrial wealth of South Wales over the last two hundred years or so has been significant. In fact, the area's industrial beginnings go back much further: in 1584 one of the first copper smelters to be built in Wales was established at Aberdulais Falls.

Local mining of ironstone also encouraged the growth of ironmaking, with charcoal used for smelting. Eventually ore was imported from Cornwall and shipped up the River Nedd as far as Aberdulais, and the problem of transporting ore and iron products led to the development of two canals. The Neath Canal opened in 1795 and the Tennant Canal in 1824, the latter giving a vital direct link with the docks at Swansea.

By the early 1800's the Melin-y-Cwrt Ironworks, just south of Resolven, was in production, followed in 1842 by the Venallt Ironworks. The trade in ores from Cornwall also attracted a group of Quaker industrialists, who established an ironworks at Neath Abbey. In 1851 came another major change – the arrival of the railways, carried by some of Brunel's most magnificent viaducts.

The Neath area has strong connections with other eminent Victorians. Tregelles Price, dedicated to the abolition of slavery and capital punishment, founded the Peace Society. William Weston Young (1776-1847) owned a brickworks at Pontwalby, Glynneath. He developed the Dinas firebrick – a product of exceptional quality, made from silica, which could withstand very high temperatures. The silica was mined locally until the early part of this century. And it was biologist Alfred Russell Wallace (1823-1918) who coined the phrase "natural selection", having developed the theory of evolution quite independently of Darwin. However, they did work together and in 1858 presented a joint paper on the subject to the Linnean Society.

### Waterfall Country

In the Vale of Neath there are more waterfalls concentrated into one small area than in any other part of Wales. The best-known and most accessible falls are those at Melincourt and Aberdulais, as well as the seventeen enchanting cascades created at Gnoll Country Park, Neath, by Herbert Mackworth in 1740.

Many more waterfalls are to be found in the wooded valleys and deep gorges of the rivers Mellte, Hepste and Nedd, between the villages of Pontneddfechan and Ystradfellte, on the southern edge of the Brecon Beacons. The only way to see them is on foot, and the car park of the Angel Inn in Pontneddfechan is the ideal starting point.

The easiest of the walks from here is to the falls at Sgwd Gwladus. Some of the other eight falls in the area can be more difficult to get to, particularly in wet and slippery conditions, and the National Park Authority points out that visitors should be aware of the potential hazards presented by such a spectacular landscape. The Authority, which has produced a useful leaflet entitled *Waterfall Walks in the Ystradfellte Area,* also recommends that you should not attempt to explore the falls unless properly dressed and equipped for walking. Another informative publication is the full-colour booklet *Waterfall Walks in the Vale of Neath,* while the Ordnance Survey Outdoor Leisure Map Number 11 (republished in a new edition in spring 1996 as Number 12) is an invaluable aid to serious walkers in the area.

The nine falls in the Pontneddfechan area are Sgwd Gwladys and Sgwd Einion Gam on the River Pyrddin; Horseshoe Falls, Lower Ddwli Falls and Upper Ddwli Falls on the Neddfechan River; the Sgwd-yr-Eira Falls on the River Hepste; and the falls of Lower, Middle and Upper Clungwyn on the River Mellte.

Each is spectacular in its own way, and if revisited at different times of the year rewards you with new aspects of its natural beauty as the changing seasons alter the face and colour of the landscape.

### Aberdulais Falls

Owned by the National Trust and one of the most famous waterfalls in the Vale of Neath, Aberdulais is set in a picturesque wooded gorge and is important for its industrial archaeology. Water has been harnessed here since 1584 to provide power for a variety of industries. The new hydro-electric Turbine House gives visitors access to the top of the falls, and nearby is Britain's largest electricity-generating waterwheel, over 26 feet in diameter – a replica of the 1830's original which drove the rolling mills. There is also a Visitor Information Centre. For more details ring 01639 636674.

### Melincourt Falls

Located just outside Resolven, Melincourt Waterfalls Reserve is owned and managed by Glamorgan

Wildlife Trust. The spectacular falls, on a tributary of the River Neath, are 80 feet high and were captured on canvas by Turner in 1794. The reserve itself includes 12 acres of broad-leaved woodland, and in spring the woodland floor is a carpet of bluebells. This humid narrow valley is also home to an interesting variety of birds, including redstart, wood warbler, pied flycatcher, dipper and grey wagtail.

### Gnoll Country Park
The gardens of Gnoll Park, the most important 18th-century landscaped gardens in Wales, are open free of charge during daylight hours. Of the many interesting and enchanting features here, the most impressive are the seventeen cascades, rushing down the hill into the Mosshouse reservoir. There is also a Visitor Centre (free admission) and a cafe, the latter overlooking the water. For more information ring 01639 635808.

### Neath Abbey
This Cistercian abbey was founded in 1130 on a rocky terrace overlooking the river marshlands. It became one of the richest of all Welsh monasteries, acquiring very extensive land and property holdings, large numbers of sheep, horses and cattle, and commercial interests which included shipping, mills, fisheries and coal mines. But by the 1530's only eight monks remained here, and after the Dissolution of the Monasteries by Henry VIII in 1536 the abbey was vandalised and fell into disuse and decay. In the 18th century it was converted into a large mansion. Part of the abbey was even used as a furnace for a copperworks. The abbey, standing on the banks of the Tennant Canal, is open all year round.

### Neath Museum
Occupying two Grade II listed buildings – Gwyn Hall and Church Place Mechanics' Institute, both in the heart of the town – this outstanding museum is open all year round and depicts the area's fascinating historical, industrial, archaeological and cultural heritage. For more information ring 01639 645726 or 645741.

### Neath Fair
The oldest and biggest fair of its kind in Wales, Neath Fair is an exciting and colourful 4-day event. It is held twice a year – at Easter and in September.

### Neath Canal, Resolven
Together the Neath and Tennant Canals form a 21-

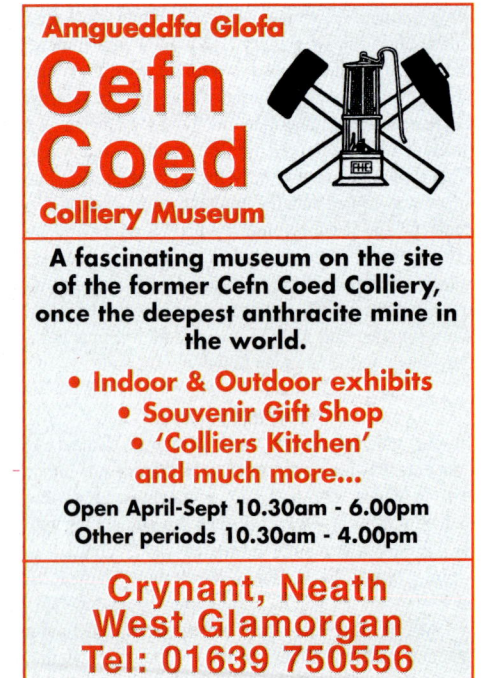

---

**The Princess Royal Theatre**

*Entertainment to suit all tastes*

Concerts · Dinner Dances
Wedding Receptions
Pantomime · Choirs
Arts & Crafts Exhibitions
Ballet · Flower Shows etc

Civic Centre, Port Talbot
West Glamorgan SA13 1PJ
Contact Mr Andrew Eagle on 01792 222601

---

**Amgueddfa Glofa Cefn Coed Colliery Museum**

A fascinating museum on the site of the former Cefn Coed Colliery, once the deepest anthracite mine in the world.

- Indoor & Outdoor exhibits
- Souvenir Gift Shop
- 'Colliers Kitchen'
and much more...

Open April-Sept 10.30am - 6.00pm
Other periods 10.30am - 4.00pm

**Crynant, Neath West Glamorgan Tel: 01639 750556**

mile waterway between Glynneath and Swansea. A 4-mile stretch of the Neath Canal above Resolven has been restored, and the landscaped towpath provides a very pleasant countryside walk taking in 7 locks, 2 aqueducts, 4 bridges, and canal basins at both Resolven and Aberdulais. Other attractions include summer barge trips from Resolven. For more information ring 01792 222790.

### Penscynor Wildlife Park

Award-winning Penscynor has earned an international reputation for its conservation work, and particularly for the care and captive breeding of endangered parrots, primates and other species. It also has many attractions other than animals which make this a great family day out.

The park is involved in numerous international initiatives for species conservation. High on the agenda are primates, such as the golden lion tamarins, some of which have been born and reared in the park and subsequently released into their native Brazilian forests. The success of the reptile breeding programme has also seen Round Island skinks returned to Mauritius as part of the plan to reintroduce them to their original habitat. Penscynor also supports several international field projects, such as trying to protect the wildlife and ecology of the Colombian rainforest, and has an Education Department and a full-time Education Officer. The idea of formal teaching for school groups has now evolved into a more active approach to informing and educating all the park's visitors by means of animal-handling sessions, question and answer sessions, feeding-time talks and so on. You can also play your part in conservation by adopting an animal at the park. For more information about the park and its many attractions ring 01639 642189.

### Gunsmoke Cowboy Town & Seven Sisters Sawmill and Museum

This award-winning double attraction is in the Dulais Valley, 11 miles north of Neath, on the A4109. The miniature cowboy town of Gunsmoke is a sheer delight for children, while at Honeysuckle Grove the houses are three-quarters normal size. There is also plenty to see in the Seven Sisters Sawmill and Museum. For more information ring 01639 700288.

### Cefn Coed Colliery Museum

The museum, near Crynant in the Dulais Valley, stands on the site of what was the world's deepest anthracite mine. On show is the massive steam

---

## AQUADOME
### AT THE AFAN LIDO · PORT TALBOT

**Discover** a place where the ancient incas met visitors from another world, where there's **thrills** and **excitement**, the sounds and sights of space travel and the jungle, all making an exciting family fun day out.

Britain's **newest** and most **adventurous** leisure theme pool can provide something for everyone, both young and old!

**BARS & RESTAURANTS   WAVE MACHINE   TOWERING FALLS   SPACE WHIRL
INCA TEMPLE   WATER SLIDES   FIBER OPTICS   FREE CAR PARK**

**OPEN 7 DAYS A WEEK - ASK FOR DETAILS OF SPECIAL FAMILY RATES**
only just off the M4, a world of excitement

**AFAN LIDO · ABERAVON SEAFRONT · PORT TALBOT
TEL: 01639 871444 (8 LINES) · FAX: 01639 893203**

winding engine which once lowered and raised the cages in the shaft, and there is an underground mining gallery, exhibition area and outdoor exhibits. For more information ring 01639 750556.

### Old gunpowder factory and the Dinas Silica Mines, Pontneddfechan

The area around the village of Pontneddfechan was once a thriving centre of industry and innovation. The Gunpowder Works, located on the banks of the River Mellte, was established in 1857 by the Vale of Neath Powder Company and later merged with the explosives company of the Swedish chemist and engineer Alfred Bernhard Nobel – the inventor of dynamite and founder of the Nobel prizes. Silica rock, or quartzite, was mined commercially in the area from the late 18th century until 1964. The silica mines stood near Dinas Rock, where the quartzite was first discovered in the 1780's. Just 2 miles away was the Pontwalby Brickworks, which manufactured the famous Dinas silica fire-brick.

### Craig Gwladus Country Park

Lying between Penscynor Wildlife Park and Neath golf course, the park gives spectacular views over the Dulais and lower Neath valleys. Attractions include an extensive area of woodland, waymarked footpaths, picnic areas, and a great variety of birds, including woodpecker, tree-creeper, nuthatch, sparrowhawk, buzzard and barn owl. The park is open free during daylight hours.

### Eaglesbush Valley

A tranquil woodland area along a river valley which provides a green and pleasant walk within the densely populated area of Melincrythan. It is open free during daylight hours.

*Black Mountains*

### Pant-y-Sais Fen

This is an SSSI (Site of Special Scientific Interest) and also a designated Nature Reserve. It is situated in the centre of the village of Jersey Marine, and a car park and boardwalks give access to the fenland. It is open free during daylight hours.

### Tairgwaith Trotting Track

Situated near Gwaun Cae Gurwen, this is one of only two hard-surface tracks in Wales and hosts nine race meetings a year. The highlight is the August Bank Holiday event. For more information ring 01269 823288.

### Dan-Yr-Ogof Showcaves

A major tourist attraction, the showcave complex is the largest in Western Europe and is located midway between Swansea and Brecon on the A4067, within the Brecon Beacons National Park. The winner of no less than 10 important tourism awards, the showcaves boast many unique features, including the longest showcave in Britain, the largest single chamber in any British showcave, and the Bone Cave (home of Bronze Age man 3000 years ago). There are many other attractions, and nearby is the Craig-y-Nos Country Park. For more information ring 01639 730284 or 730693.

---

Joan & Nicola welcome you to

## Old White Horse Inn

Runner-up Welsh Village Pub of The Year 1993
In the middle of Pontneddfechan.
Enjoy home cooked food and a pint of real ale.
Vegetarian meals available. Lunches & Evening Meals Served Daily. Tea Rooms and Self Catering Accommodation

HIGH STREET,
PONTNEDDFECHAN,
NR GLYNNEATH, SA11 5NP
Tel: (01639) 721219

# Port Talbot & the Afan Valley

Just a mile from Port Talbot is Aberavon, which for decades has been popular with day trippers and holidaymakers who enjoy its wide sandy beach. More than two miles long and safe for bathing, it is well patronised by surfers, windsurfers, canoeists and other watersport enthusiasts. At one end it stretches to the Neath estuary, at the other to Port Talbot docks; beyond the docks is the even longer spread of Margam Sands.

Backing Aberavon beach is the promenade and its variety of attractions – sunken gardens, boating and paddling pools, play equipment, and easy parking just 50 yards from the sands. Ambitious plans are in hand for major redevelopment of Aberavon seafront, including an extensive coastal protection scheme, and the Afan Lido has been transformed into a state-of-the-art leisure complex. It was re-opened in spring 1996 and one of its star attractions is the fabulous new

*Margam Park*

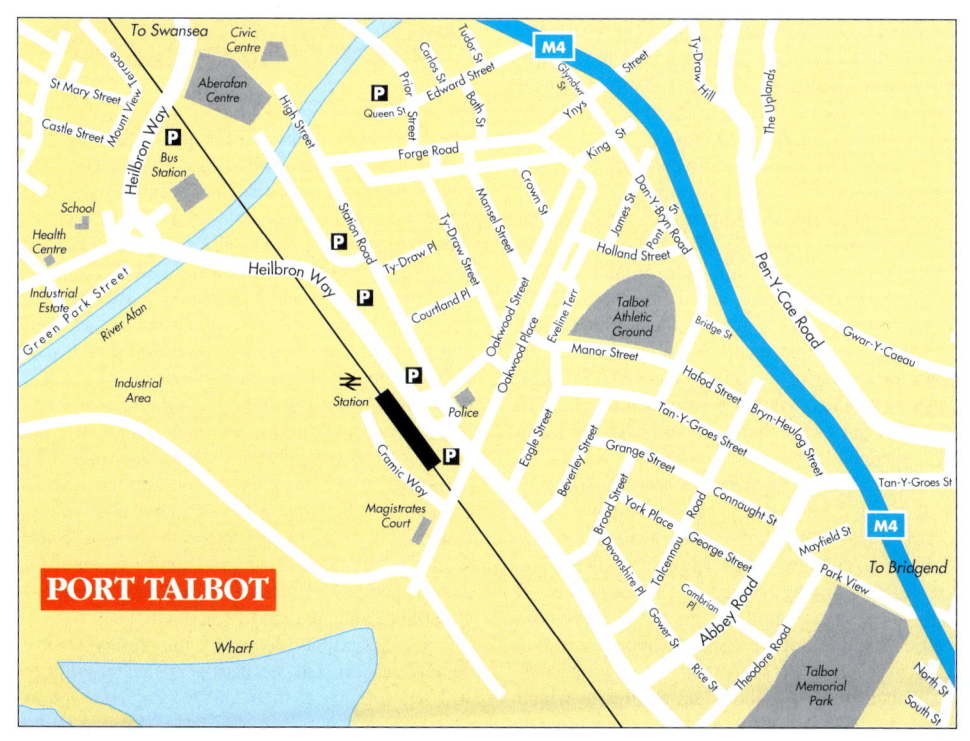

Aqua Dome – a water park which incorporates a themed pool and a host of exciting new features and activities.

The other attractions within easy reach of Port Talbot could hardly provide a more striking contrast to the urban and industrial landscape. The beautiful Afan Valley, one of the most picturesque valleys in Wales, is a real breath of fresh air in every sense. An excellent starting point for exploring its great natural beauty is the Countryside Centre in the Afan Argoed Country Park. From here you can see the valley by any number of means – on foot, horseback, bike or Landrover. Another country park well worthy of a visit is Margam Park, where the castle was once the home of the Talbot family who gave their name to the port.

The history of the Port Talbot area can be traced back at least 4000 years. There is evidence of occupation here in the Neolithic Age, and traces of Bronze Age and Iron Age tumuli and hillforts can be seen at Mynydd y Gaer (Baglan), Pen-y-Castell (Ynysygwas), and Bwlwarcau (North Margam). The discovery of four inscribed stones is also proof that a Roman road ran through what is now Port Talbot, and other important historical finds include two 6th-century stones with Ogham characters which are in the Stones Museum at Margam Abbey. The great Wheel Cross of Conbelin is also in the museum, along with other Celtic stones and crosses.

A seaport for hundreds of years and known as Port Aberavon until the 19th century, Port Talbot saw the beginning of two centuries of industrial growth with the opening of a copper-smelting works in 1770. Copper ore was shipped in from the nearby Cornish coast, and the area around the harbour grew at such a pace that it soon became a town in its own right. In 1836 it was renamed Port Talbot in honour of the Talbot family of Margam Castle – pioneers of the booming industry, and owners of most of the land on which the town and docks were built.

Further prosperity arrived with the railway revolution. Coal exports grew and the port became a major distribution point for many of the coalmining villages of the Rhondda Valley. The Port Talbot Railway opened in 1897, followed in 1898 by a new modern dock to serve the coalfields and to import iron and copper.

It was not until 1946 that a steelworks was established in Port Talbot – an enterprise which brought welcome relief from the effects of mine closures in the Afan and surrounding valleys. By 1970 this had become the largest steelworks in Britain and today is one of the most modern in Europe.

Port Talbot's importance as an industrial centre and major port was further underlined in the 1970's with the commissioning of Britain's biggest deep-water harbour. This now provides the deepest berthing facility in the Bristol Channel and can comfortably accommodate vessels well in excess of 100,000 tons.

Despite its industry, the Port Talbot area is still largely rural and the economy is dominated by the town and its suburbs of Baglan, Aberavon, Taibach and Margam. The town centre, much of which was late Victorian and early Edwardian, has been redeveloped on both sides of the River Afan. On the west bank is the Civic Centre, which houses the Princess Royal Theatre – an important venue for a wide variety of international entertainment, fashion shows and other major events.

## The Afan Valley

The winding and picturesque Afan is the narrowest of all the Welsh mining valleys. The river is only twelve miles long, rising west of the Rhondda Valley and snaking its way down to Aberavon to merge with the waters of Swansea Bay and the Bristol Channel.

From the early 19th century until the late 1960's, the Afan Valley was famous for its coal and for the railways which carried it to the docks at Port Talbot. The last mine closed in 1971. Since then the hillsides laid barren by mining operations have been replanted, and large areas of new coniferous woodland have earned the valley the name of Little Switzerland. The similarities are clear to see: forested hills, the steep-sided valley, fast-flowing streams and panoramic views. Such scenic beauty is a miracle of land reclamation, and the network of forestry tracks makes it easy to experience and appreciate it first hand.

Yet not all evidence of the valley's long dependence on coal has disappeared. The villages still retain much of their unique character, and at

Afan Valley

# Margam Country Park
### Port Talbot, West Glamorgan

## There's plenty to do and see at Margam Country Park

- 800 acre Country Estate to explore
- Plenty of car parking space
- Historic Orangery, Abbey &Castle
- Mother and toddler play area
- Bouncing Castle
- Boating
- Giant Chess and Draughts
- Putting
- Farm trail and Pets corner
- Refreshments
- Ranger service and Guided walks
- Easy access off the M4
- Crown Jewels Exhibition
- Formal gardens
- Children's Fairytale Land
- Adventure Playground
- Margam Maze
- Road Train rides
- Deer herd
- Sculpture displays
- Gift Shop
- Full programme of Events

*. . . a complete Day Out for All the Family*

## Opening Times

**1st April to 30th September**
Attractions open 10am -5.30pm · Country Park open 10am - 7pm
Last entry to Park 4pm and to attractions 5pm

**1st October to 31st March**
Country Park only · open Wednesdays to Sundays 10am - 5pm
Last entry to Park 3pm

**Dogs** are permitted to enter the Country Park on condition that they are kept on a lead and under strict control at all times. Dogs are not permitted in or on any of the Park's attractions.

Telephone Park Office: 01639 881635
Recorded Information: 01639 871131
Fax No: 01639 895897
Correspondence: The Park Director, Margam Park, Port Talbot Sa13 2TJ

Cymmer there is a permanent reminder of the valley's once-extensive railway network, the refreshment room of the old station having been converted into a pub.

One son of the valley who exchanged a working life at the coal face for a glittering career on stage and film was the late Richard Burton. He was born in the village of Pontrhydyfen, where the valley is so constricted that viaducts and aqueducts provided the only routes by which coal could be transported.

### Afan Argoed Country Park & Welsh Miners Museum

Set in acres of unspoiled woodland, the park is the gateway to exploring the Afan Valley. There are plenty of waymarked footpaths, including the 27-mile Coed Morgannwg Way, which links the park with Margam Park and Rhigos mountain. There is also a wayfaring/orienteering course and the far less strenuous riverside walk. You can hire a mountain bike and escape along any of the 14 miles of bike routes, which are mainly off road and take you through beautiful countryside. Another alternative is to hop aboard the Landrover and enjoy spectacular views as you trek through the forests.

Focal point of the park is the Countryside Centre. The building also houses the Welsh Miners Museum, which gives a vivid portrayal of what life was like for the men and children who toiled deep underground in the valley's pits, and of the hardships endured by the small mining communities.

Other facilities in the park include picnic sites, a barbecue area, an adventure playground, camping, and a small touring caravan site. The park is six miles north-east of Port Talbot on the A4107 (exit 40 M4) and is open all year. For more information ring 01639 850564.

### Margam Country Park

Only two miles east of Port Talbot, historic Margam Park is a major attraction and comprises 850 acres of open parkland and forest. Among its ancient sites are a 7-acre Iron Age hillfort and the ruins of 12th-century Margam Abbey. Then there is Margam Castle – a Tudor/Gothic-style mansion house completed in 1840 for the Talbot family – and the magnificent 18th-century Orangery, constructed originally to house orange trees. The park is also notable for its collection of work by internationally-renowned sculptors, and for its maze – one of the largest in the world. The wildlife population includes 600 deer and a herd of rare Glamorgan cattle. The park's many other attractions and activities – Fairytaleland, pony rides, pony trekking, the Coach House Theatre and a great deal more – make for a very full day out. For more information ring 01639 881635.

### Wildlife & the countryside

The wooded valleys, open moorland, forestry plantations, sand dunes and parkland of the Port Talbot area provide many opportunities to enjoy the countryside. Remnants of the Afan Valley's original oak and birch woodlands can still be seen, with a rich variety of birds, plants and animals, and newer plantations are attracting their own characteristic birds. In winter, Eglwys Nunydd Reservoir and the Kenfig Nature Reserve are important feeding grounds for wildfowl.

More about the area's wildlife can be learned from the Afan Argoed Countryside Centre and the Field Studies Centre in Margam Park.

---

**Afan FOREST PARK**
**Countryside Centre & Miners' Museum**

9,000 acres of forest have been specially set aside by the Forest Enterprise for you to explore and enjoy.
For quiet relaxation, walking, pony trekking or cycling...
come to Afan Forest Park.
The South Wales Miners' Museum gives a fascinating insight into the social history of the Valley's mining communities
The 'Wayfarers' Rest' cafe and a basic camping/caravan site is available at the Countryside Centre.

**For more details telephone**
**01639 850564**

# Porthcawl & Ogwr

Porthcawl has been established as a popular seaside resort since the days when the mining communities around Bridgend and the Rhondda valleys first started coming here for their holidays. Today's visitors come in greater numbers and from much further afield, drawn by a growing awareness that beyond Porthcawl's beaches and attractions is an area of outstanding beauty and interest.

This is Ogwr – a compact district boasting a landscape which varies from towering cliffs and sprawling sand dunes to deep valleys and forested mountains. Equally diverse is the number and scope of its visitor attractions. You can enjoy the beaches of Porthcawl and Southerndown, ride the fun fair of the Coney Beach complex, take in the spectacular cliff scenery of the Heritage Coast, participate in golf or fishing or watersports, get away from it all in the seclusion of Bryngarw Country Park, and take a 15-mile drive north from the coast and suddenly find yourself on dramatic mountain roads a world apart from the lively holiday atmosphere of Porthcawl.

The all-weather recreational facilities in Ogwr are outstanding too, including the largest leisure centre in South Wales and seven indoor swimming pools. Of the district's five top-class golf courses, the Royal Porthcawl is the most famous – one of the best-known links courses in Britain.

And should all of this fail to whet your appetite for Ogwr, there are historic sites and castles, craft workshops, nature reserves and interesting towns and villages.

The resort of Porthcawl grew around the little harbour towards the end of the 19th century, tending to the holiday needs of miners from nearby valleys. The harbour itself existed only because of the coal

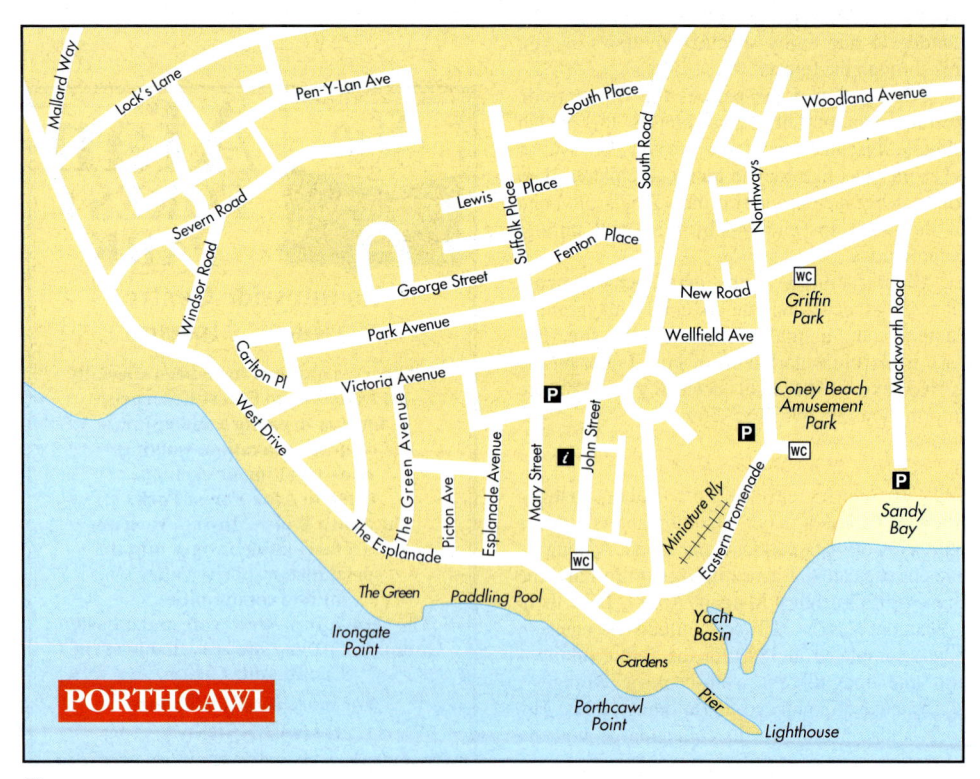

*Ogmore-by-Sea*

industry. Trade was at its peak in 1873 but declined with the opening of new docks at Barry and Port Talbot. By 1907 it had ceased altogether.

Nearly a century on, the picturesque harbour is busy with fishermen and pleasure boats, and sandy Porthcawl has become the most popular spot in Ogwr. Very much a family resort, its appeal has been boosted still further by an attractive new promenade and pedestrianisation of the main shopping area in John Street. The wide choice of accommodation includes one of Europe's best holiday home parks – virtually a resort in its own right – where the activities and attractions are open to everyone.

Sandy Bay and Trecco Bay have safe golden beaches, the latter boasting a superb new leisure pool. Then there is the huge Coney Beach Pleasure Park. In the summer of 1996 a new road train rolls into operation, providing trips around the resort and linking all the amenities and attractions.

With a shoreline ideally suited to watersports, and night-time entertainment provided by clubs, discos and the Grand Pavilion theatre, lively Porthcawl is a hive of holiday fun. Yet to the west of the esplanade you can discover the peace and quiet of Lock's Common and the secluded sands and rock pools of appropriately-named Rest Bay. The beaches of this popular surfing venue extend beyond the links of the 18-hole Royal Porthcawl Golf Club to Sker Point. Here you will find Sker House – a local landmark elevated to fame by R.D. Blackmore's 1872 novel *The Maid of Sker*.

Porthcawl is often described as sandy – and not

just because of its three superb beaches. The vast sand dunes of Kenfig Burrows lie to the west and Merthyr Mawr Warren to the east. The picturesque village of Merthyr Mawr, with its charming thatched cottages, lies on the edge of what is one of the biggest areas of dunes in Britain. Iron Age and other important archaeological finds have been made here, many of which are on display in the National Museum of Wales in Cardiff. A network of footpaths criss-crosses the dunes, which are an important wildlife habitat and a Site of Special Scientific Interest. Standing among the dunes are the sparse ruins of Candleston Castle.

Beyond Merthyr Mawr is the village of Ogmore-by-Sea – another popular holiday spot, nestling on the rocky shoreline of the Ogmore estuary. From here the coastline to the east rises up to spectacular towering cliffs, where one of the few breaks in the 14-mile stretch of precipitous Glamorgan Heritage Coast occurs at Southerndown's Dunraven Bay.

This attractive sheltered beach offers safe bathing and good surfing and has made Southerndown a popular little resort. From the Heritage Coast Visitor Centre you can explore Dunraven Park – 56 acres of sloping grasslands which were part of the estate of the now-demolished Dunraven Castle.

Five miles east of Porthcawl is medieval Bridgend, the largest town in Ogwr and outstanding for its shopping and leisure facilities. Another town of interest is Maesteg, where it is said that Richard Burton made his acting debut on the stage of the town hall.

### Coney Beach Pleasure Park, Porthcawl
All the fun of the fair, with a big choice of great rides and amusements overlooking the beach. For more information ring 01656 713111.

### Grand Pavilion, Porthcawl
A popular seafront venue for summer shows and a wide variety of entertainment throughout the year. For more information ring 01656 716996.

### Porthcawl Museum
Located in John Street, this small museum has interesting displays of geological specimens, costumes and memorabilia of old Porthcawl. For more information ring 01656 712211.

### Kenfig Pool & Dunes National Nature Reserve
The sand dunes of the Kenfig Burrows and the reserve's 70-acre freshwater pool provide an important habitat for a variety of wildlife. For more information ring 01656 743386.

### Bryngarw Country Park
A few miles from the centre of Bridgend, this secluded park is characterised by open meadows, thick woodland, immaculate gardens, ornamental lakelands and riverside walks. There is also a Visitor Centre. For more information ring 01656 725155.

### Ogmore Castle
Standing beside the River Ewenny, the castle was a strategic Norman stronghold guarding an important crossing point – part of a triangle of defences on the fertile Vale of Glamorgan.

### Ewenny Pottery
The oldest working pottery in Wales, founded in 1610. For more information ring 01656 653020.

### Ewenny Priory
An unusual fortified 12th-century religious settlement, founded in 1141, which looks more like a castle than an abbey. It is considered to be one of the best examples of its kind in Britain.

### Coity Castle, Bridgend
Dating from the 14th century, this extensive ruin of an important medieval Norman stronghold is two miles north-east of the town centre.

### Newcastle Castle, Bridgend
The remains of this Norman castle boast an exceptionally well-preserved south gateway, which is also notable for its richly-carved decoration. The castle stands on a hill overlooking the town and river.

### Glamorgan Nature Centre
Close to Bridgend, the Centre is the headquarters of Glamorgan Wildlife Trust and is rich in flora and fauna. The Trust, a registered charity, now manages 46 reserves totalling nearly 1400 acres, and membership enables you to contribute to important conservation work. For more information ring 01656 724100.

# The Great Sporting & Activity Holiday

Those visitors in search of an active holiday will not be disappointed in this corner of Wales. Here is a brief guide to some of the many sports and recreational facilities available throughout the Swansea Bay region. Further information is available from the local Tourist Information Centres listed on page 69.

### Akido
Llanelli is the home of the Welsh Aikido Association, which holds an annual summer school at Burry Port. You can also participate at the YMCA, Llanelli (01554 774898).

### Birdwatching
The Swansea Bay region is ideal for birdwatching, the diverse and beautiful scenery creating a variety of habitats for many different species. Areas of particular interest are Mumbles Hill (Local Nature Reserve), Black Pill (on the shoreline near Mumbles), Bishops Wood Nature Reserve (Caswell Bay, Gower), Oxwich National Nature Reserve (Gower), Worms Head National Nature Reserve (Gower), Whiteford Reserve (Burry Inlet, Loughor estuary), the Wildfowl & Wetlands Centre (near Llanelli) and Pant-y-sais Fen (Jersey Marine). For more details refer to the free booklet, *Birdwatching in and around Swansea*, available from the city's Tourist Information Centre.

### Boating
Neath Canal: boats up to 500mm draft can be accommodated (017 222730).

### Bowling (10-pin)
GX Superbowl, Swansea (01792 467364).

### Bowls
Port Talbot & Afan Valley and Vale of Neath (01792 222565)
Burry Port Memorial Park (01554 834497).
Griffin Park Bowling Greens, Porthcawl.
Parc Howard, Llanelli (01554 770929).
Parc Stephens, Kidwelly (01554 891046).
People's Park, Llanelli.
Selwyn Samuel Centre, Llanelli (01554 776506).
Swansea area: over 15 outdoor greens (01792 302411).

### Canoeing
Neath Canal at Resolven, and at Glynconwg Ponds.
Pembrey Country Park.
Lliedi Reservoir.
Sandy Water Park, Llanelli (canoe hire available).
Kidwelly Quay (canoe hire available).

### Cricket
Cricket clubs: Baglan (01639 812797); BP Llandarcy (01792 812036); British Steel Port Talbot (01639 882066); Briton Ferry Steel (01639 823085); Briton Ferry Town (01639 812227); Cimla (01639 637736); Cwmgwrach (01639 883898); Dyffryn (01639 812187); Margam (01639 885500); Pontardawe (01639 862228); Port Talbot Town (01639 897288); Skewen (01792 813757); Ynysygerwn (01639 642547); Ystalyfera (01639 842972); Llanelli Cricket Club (01554 773721); Neath Cricket Club, The Gnoll (01639 643719); Swansea Cricket Club (01792 464918).

### Cycling
**Afan Valley**: bikes for hire from Afan Argoed Countryside Centre (01639 850564).
**M&P Cycles**: established in Swansea for 5 years and offering Wales' largest selection of cycles and accessories. Main dealers for Raleigh, Falcon, Dawes, Claud Butler, Specialized and Trek, M&P have two branches – one in St. Helen's Road, city centre, and the other on the Enterprise Park at Llansamlet. Both are easily accessible via the Swansea cycle path network. Full workshop facilities are available at both branches, as is cycle hire throughout the year. The range caters for all shapes, sizes and pockets. In fact, everything you need to go cycling on Gower is right here. For more information ring 01792 702555/644204
**Pembrey Country Park**: bike hire available during summer (01554 833913).
**Swansea Bay and area**: offers cyclists many opportunities, including the Swansea Bikepath and Tawe Riverside Path, with bike hire available at several places. For more details refer to the free booklet, *Cycling in and around Swansea*, available

*The Premier Guide to Swansea Bay & Gower*

from the city's Tourist Information Centre.

## Fishing
**Llanelli area**
Burry Port: boat hire & trips available
Burry Port Fishing Festival.
Glynconwg Ponds.
Llanelli: Furnace Pond & Swiss Valley Reservoir
**Swansea Bay**
The bay boasts some of the best angling grounds off Britain's coast, and hire-boat skippers know the most productive areas. Cod, bass, monkfish (rock salmon) and mackerel are among the most common catches. For more information contact Swansea Angling Centre (01792 469999). Mumbles Pier is also popular with fishermen. Other venues within Swansea require permits, available from the city council's Fishing Permits Office (01792 302411).
**Vale of Neath**
Game fishing is available in the Neath and Dulais rivers, and coarse fishing in the Neath and Tennant canals and Gnoll Park grounds. For other venues contact:
Glynneath & District Angling Association
(01639 720927).

Neath & District Angling Association
(01639 701187).

## Flying
Contact Swansea Airport (01792 204063).

## Golf
Ashburnham Golf Club, Burry Port
(01554 832269).
Blackpill Golf Course, Swansea (01792 207544).
Earlswood Golf Course, Jersey Marine
(01792 321578).
Glynclydach House Hotel (01639 818411).
Glynneath Golf Club, near Pontneddfechan
(01639 720452).
Gnoll Park, Neath (01639 641121).
Gower Golf Course & Club (01792 872480).
Gowerton Golf Range. See also page 46.
(01792 875188).
Lakeside Golf Club, Margam (01639 883486).
Maesteg Golf Club (01656 732037).
Neath Golf Course (01639 643615).
Palleg Golf Club, Lower Cwmtwrch (01639 842193).
Pembrey Pitch & Putt, Pembrey Country Park
(01554 833913).
Pontardawe Golf Club (01792 863118).
Pontnewydd Golf Centre, Trimsaran
(01554 810278).
Pyle and Kenfig Golf Club (01656 713093).
Royal Porthcawl Golf Club (01656 712251).
Southerndown Golf Club (01656 880326).
St. Mary's Hill Golf Club, Pencoed
(01656 864720).
Swansea Bay Golf Course, Jersey Marine
(01792 812198).
Tycroes Golf Range (01269 596460).

---

**M&P CYCLES**

- 1,000's of bikes to choose from
- Massive range of accessories and clothing to suit every need
- Full range of childrens bikes
- Adult Mountain Bikes from £89.95
- Full workshop facilities
- Cycle hire available

**Opening Times:**
Mon - Sat, 9.00am to 6.00pm (Both Branches)
Sun 11am to 5pm
(Enterprise Park only)

Unit 3/4 Castell Close,
Swansea Enterprise Park, Swansea
Tel: 01792 702555 Fax: 01792 700396
and
31 St Helens Road, Swansea
Tel: 01792 644204 Fax: 01792 644204

---

**MIKE DAVIES LEISURE LTD**

For all your Caravan, Camping & Marine Accessories
Tents, Awnings, Clothing and Ski Wear

EVERYTHING FOR TODAY'S OUTDOOR FAMILY

665 Gower Road, Upper Killay, Swansea
**Tel: (01792) 203177/208954**
Follow the signs to Swansea Airport

*The Great Sporting & Activity Holiday*

### *Hangliding*
Contact WLA, Swansea Airport (01792 464073).

### *Horse Riding & Pony Trekking*
Cimla Trekking Holiday & Equestrian Centre
 (01639 644944).
Clyn-Du Riding Centre, Pembrey Mountain
(01554 832546).
Equestrian Centre, Pembrey Country Park
(01554 832160).
Hawdref Ganol Farm, Cimla (01639 631884).
L&A Riding Centre (01639 885509).
Mid Glamorgan Riding Club, Heol-y-Cyw,
near Bridgend (01656 862959).
Moss House Reservoir, Tonna (01639 630836).
Pant-y-Sais Riding Centre, Jersey Marine
(01792 813213 or 816439).
Parc-le-Breos Riding & Holiday Centre
(01792 371636).
Pitton Cross Trekking Centre (01792 390554).

### *Karting*
Circuit Scene, Pembrey Circuit:
kart hire available. (01554 891455).
Supertrax Go Kart Centre, Swansea
(01792 775551).

### *Kite Buggying*
Pembrey Country Park (01554 833913).

### *Land Yachting*
Cefan Sidan Land Yacht Club (01554 832022).

### *Motorsports and Racing Driving*
The Welsh Motorsports Centre, Pembrey:
racing, tuition, karting and rallying
(01554 891455).

### *Orienteering*
Pembrey Country Park (01554 833913).

### *Outdoor Pursuits*
Clyne Farm Activity Centre (01792 403333).
Pelenna Mountain Centre (01639 636227).
Rhossili Outdoor Education Centre
(01792 401548).

### *Paragliding*
Contact WLA, Swansea Airport
(01792 464073).

*Ski Centre, Pembrey Country Park*

### *Rugby*
Aberavon Quins RFC (01639 884612).
Aberavon RFC, Talbot Athletic Ground
(01639 882434).
Glynneath RFC, Abernant Park (01639 720442).
Llanelli RFC, Stradey Park (01554 774060).
Neath RFC, The Gnoll (01639 636547).
Resolven RFC (01639 710210).
Seven Sisters RFC, Maes Dafydd.
Tonmawr RFC, Whitworth Grounds (01639 642948).
Swansea RFC (01792 642381).

### *Sailing*
Monkstone Marina, Briton Ferry (01792 812229).
Mumbles Sailing School (01792 362265).
Rainbow Sailing (01792 467813).
Swansea Marina (01792 470310).

### *Ski-ing*
Pembrey Country Park (01554 834443).
Swansea Ski Centre (01792 645639 or 367321).

### *Snooker*
Terry Griffiths Matchroom, Riley Snooker Club,
Llanelli (01554 774494).

65

*The Premier Guide to Swansea Bay & Gower*

## Soccer
Llanelli AFC, Stebonheath (01554 772973).
Swansea City FC, Vetch Field (01792 462584).

## Sports & Leisure Centres
Afan Lido Leisure Complex & AquaDome, Aberavon (01639 871444)
Bridgend Recreation Centre (01656 657491).
Garw Valley Centre, Pontycymer (01656 870886).
Llanelli Leisure Centre (01554 756249).
Maesteg Sports Centre (01656 737121).
Morfa Stadium, Swansea (01792 476578).
Neath Leisure Centre (01639 642827).
Neath Sports Centre (01639 635013).
Ogmore Valley Leisure Centre (01656 840880).
Penyrheol Leisure Centre (01792 897039).
Pyle & District Leisure Centre (01656 743712).
Swansea Leisure Centre (01792 649126).
Swansea Tennis Centre (01792 650484).

## Surfing
Contact the Welsh Surfing Federation, Porthcawl (01656 784874) and refer to the free booklet, *Surfing & Windsurfing in and around Swansea*, available from the city's Tourist Information Centre.

## Swimming Pools
Afan Lido Leisure Complex & AquaDome, Aberavon (01639 871444)
Bridgend Recreation Centre (01656 657491).
Dulais Valley Leisure Pool (01639 701584).
Glynneath Pool (01639 720460).
Gower Holiday Village (01792 390431).
Llanelli Leisure Centre (01554 774757).
Llangatwg School, Neath (01639 620230).
Llangeinor Pool (01656 870258).
Maesteg Pool (01656 733073).
Neath Leisure Centre (01639 642827).
Ogmore Vale Pool (01656 840420).
Pencoed Pool (01656 862360).
Pyle Pool (01656 744019).
Ynysawdre Pool, Tondu (01656 720806).

## Tobogganing
Pembrey Country Park (01554 834443).

## Walking
**Llanelli & area**
There are many excellent trails and footpaths, such as the Furnace Pond Trail and the Lower Lliedi Reservoir country walk, both of which are described in free leaflets available from the Tourist Information Centres in Llanelli and at Pont Abraham (listed on page 69). Pembrey Country Park also has nature trails and throughout the year offers a programme of guided walks.

**Ogwr**
Ogwr Ridgeway Walk: a dramatic 13-mile countryside path across high ground with stunning panoramic views (01656 662141).
Glamorgan Heritage Coast: spectacular views along the 14-mile coast path.

**Port Talbot & the Afan Valley**
The Port Talbot area boasts a network of forest tracks and paths. Margam Park and the Afan Argoed Country Park give access to many outstanding walks, the best-known route being the 27 miles between Margam and Craig y Llyn. The country park also has wayfaring routes laid out in conjunction with the British Orienteering Federation.

**Swansea area**
Swansea Bay and the Gower Peninsula are excellent centres for walkers. For more details of the many routes available see the free booklet, *Walking in and around Swansea*, available from the city's Tourist Information Centre.

**Vale of Neath**
Walks include the long-distance waymarked footpath Cerdded Bro Nedd (incorporating sections of the Sarn Helen Roman Road and the Coed Morgannwg) and shorter walks such as Pontneddfechan Waterfalls, Pant y Sais Fen, Melin Cwrt Falls, Neath and Tennant canals, Eaglesbush Valley, Longford Dingle, Shelone Woods and the Pelenna and Dulais valleys. For more information on all walks ring 01639 631926.

## Windsurfing
Cefn Sidan Sands, Pembrey.
Sandy Water Park, Llanelli (equipment hire available).
Refer also to the free booklet, *Surfing & Windsurfing in and around Swansea*, available from the city's Tourist Information Centre.

## Yachting
Burry Port.
Sandy Water Park, Llanelli.

# Exploring Carmarthenshire

Carmarthenshire is a veritable feast of delights and discovery – an intoxicating mix of glorious coast and countryside, where attractions range from castles, museums and art galleries to steam railways, country parks and traditional crafts.

At the heart of the county is the ancient township of Carmarthen. It stands on the River Towy, eight miles inland – a position which inspired the Romans to make it their strategic regional capital. They also built an amphitheatre here, rediscovered in 1936 but first excavated in 1968. In legend, the town is the reputed birthplace of Merlin – wizard and counsellor to King Arthur. Today it is a first-class shopping centre and a bustling market town. It is believed that the oldest manuscript in the Welsh language – *The Black Book of Carmarthen*, now in the National Library of Wales in Aberystwyth – was written in the town.

Right on Carmarthen's doorstep, at Bronwydd Arms, is the Gwili Railway – Wales' only remaining standard-gauge steam railway. There is another steam railway in the beautiful and spectacular Teifi Valley, which is rich in rural traditions and customs. Close to the market town of Newcastle Emlyn are several of the valley's other great attractions and beauty spots, notably Cilgerran Castle, the Welsh Wildlife Centre, Cenarth Falls, the National Coracle Museum, the Museum of the Welsh Woollen Industry and Henllan Falls.

South of Carmarthen, the River Towy emerges into Carmarthen Bay alongside the rivers Taf and Gwendraeth. This is an area of outstanding natural beauty, where scores of waders and seabirds take rich pickings from the broad expanse of mudflats formed by the three estuaries.

It also marks the beginning of a glorious 25-

*Brecon Beacons*

67

mile stretch of Carmarthenshire coastline. Ferryside, a charming seaside village at the mouth of the Towy, was once renowned for its cockles. On a hilltop on the opposite bank of the estuary stands the ruin of imposing Llanstephan Castle, and a short hop across the Taf estuary is Laugharne. This medieval township is where Dylan Thomas spent the latter years of his tragically short life. His home was the Boat House, now a Heritage Centre dedicated to his work. Laugharne Castle, dating from the 12th century, inspired Turner to capture it on canvas. Just west of Laugharne are the eight golden miles of Pendine Sands, famous in motorsport history as the venue for world land speed record attempts by Sir Malcolm Campbell and others in the 1920's.

The town of Whitland, on the River Taf, is also important in Welsh history. It was here in the 10th century that the great Welsh king Hywel Dda (Hywel the Good) called an assembly of wise men to draw up a unified legal code for Wales – an event now commemorated by the Hywel Dda Interpretive Gardens and Centre. To the north of the town are the scant remains of Whitland Abbey. Founded in 1140, it was the first Cistercian

*Laugharne*

monastery in Wales and gave rise to seven others, including Strata Florida.

Among Carmarthenshire's many other visitor attractions is a wide choice of sporting and leisure activities. Excellent walking country is provided by the county's cliffs, estuaries, Teifi and Towy valleys and the mystical Brechfa Forest (where a cave said to be Merlin's sits enchantingly beside a waterfall). You can also enjoy golf, watersports, pony trekking, riding and many more activities.

Carmarthenshire is particularly renowned for its fishing. The rivers Towy, Teifi, Cothi and Taf are favourite hunting grounds for anglers in search of trout, sewin and salmon. Carmarthen Bay and its estuaries, and many well-stocked trout farms and man-made pools, offer an additional challenge to the rod and line.

To find out more about places to see and things to do in the county, ring the Tourist Information Centre in Carmarthen (01267 231557) or Llanelli (01554 772020).

---

Where shall we go today?
Lets try somewhere different ~
Llandeilo has Castles, Crafts,
Countryside & Dinefwr Park.

### The Plough Inn at Rhosmaen

Enjoy Bar Meals & Afternoon Teas in the cosy Towy Lounge or on the Terrace with wonderful views of the Towy Valley & the Brecon Beacons. Try the à la carte Restaurant for Lunch, Dinner or a set Traditional Family Sunday Lunch. The panorama can also be enjoyed from all of the hotel's beautifully appointed en suite bedrooms. 1 mile from Llandeilo on A40 towards Llandovery

Llandeilo ~ (01558) 823431

# The Wales Tourist Information Centre Network

... is here to ensure that you get the very best from your holiday or day out in and around the Cardiff area.

Each centre provides:
- **PLENTY OF IDEAS FOR NEW PLACES TO VISIT AND EXPLORE**
- **INFORMATION ON BOTH LOCAL AND NATIONAL EVENTS**
- **DETAILS OF LOCAL SERVICES SUCH AS PLACES TO EAT AND BUS TIMES**
- **ASSISTANCE WITH THE PLANNING OF SCENIC ROUTES AROUND THE AREA**
- **AN EXTENSIVE SELECTION OF MAPS, GUIDES, BOOKS AND FREE LITERATURE**
- **A FREE AND INDEPENDENT LOCAL BED BOOKING SERVICE, USING ONLY THOSE ESTABLISHMENTS WHICH HAVE BEEN CHECKED OUT BY THE WALES TOURIST BOARD**

## OPEN ALL YEAR

**Bridgend TIC,** Sarn Services, Junction 36 (M4) (ring 01656 654906)
**Carmarthen TIC,** Lammas Street (ring 01267 231557)
**Llanelli TIC,** Central Library, Vaughan Street (ring 01554 772020)
**Neath TIC,** BP Sports Club, Llandarcy (ring 01792 813030)
**Pont Abraham TIC,** Junction 49 (M4) (ring 01792 883838)
**Pontneddfechan TIC,** Near Glynneath (open weekends only in winter) (ring 01639 721795)
**Swansea TIC,** Singleton Street (ring 01792 468321 or fax 01792 464602)
**Gower Peninsula:** four mini TIC's are now open, based at Mike Davies Leisure, Gower Road, Upper Killay; Shepherd's Shop, Parkmill; Treasure Trove, Port Eynon; and Heronsway Filling Station, Llanrhidian.

## OPEN ALL SUMMER

**Mumbles TIC,** Oystermouth Square, Mumbles (ring 01792 361302)
**Porthcawl TIC,** The Old Police Station, John Street (ring 01656 786639 or 782211)

## OPENING HOURS

Centres are usually open between 10.00am and 5.30pm.
To check any individual centre listed here, ring the number shown.

# Accommodation & Eating Out

**BANK FARM LEISURE PARK**, Horton, Gower, Swansea SA3 1LL. Lovely 75 acre site with excellent amenities including swimming pool, licensed bar, shop, facilities for disabled. Park Holiday Homes, Pitches for touring caravans and tents are available. Tel: 01792 390228. Fax: 01792 391282. See page 46.

**BLACKHILLS CARAVAN PARK**, Blackhills Lane, Fairwood Common, Swansea. New luxury holiday homes on 30 acre woodland caravan park. Situated on the Gower Peninsular, ideal for walks, golf, beaches, etc. Open March to December. Tel: 01792 207065. Fax: 01792 280995. See page 44.

**CJ'S WINE BAR RESTAURANT**, 135 Mumbles Road, Mumbles. Delicious menu, friendly, party atmosphere. Families welcome. Tel: 01792 361246. See page 33.

**CONWAY GUEST HOUSE**, 30 Victoria Gardens, Neath SA11 3BH. Small family run guest house situated in the centre of Neath. Colour TV and tea/coffee in all rooms. Tel: 01639 642364. See page 50.

**CWMBACH COTTAGES**, Cwmbach Road, Cadoxton, Neath SA10 8AH. In idyllic setting, surrounded by woodlands. All rooms en suite. Private car park and gardens. Tel: 01639 639825. See page 50.

**FORTE POSTHOUSE**, Kingsway Circle, Swansea. Modern, recently refurbished hotel within walking distance of Swansea Marina. 99 bedrooms, restaurant, bar, car park, indoor pool, gym, sauna and solarium. Tel: 01792 651074. Fax: 01792 456044. See page 31.

**GALLINI'S RESTAURANT**, Pilots House Wharf, Swansea Marina. Traditional Italian and fish dishes. Families and parties welcome. We also cater for Sunday Lunches £4.95 for 2 Courses 12 – 3pm. Open evenings 6pm to midnight. Tel: 01792 456285. See page 21.

**GNOLL PARK MOTEL & RESTAURANT**, 77 Cimla Road, Neath SA11 3TT. Friendly family run motel. 24 en suite bedrooms with colour TV, direct line telephone, CH and tea/coffee making facilities. Licensed bar and restaurant. Tel: 01639 645656. Fax: 01639 646284. See page 50.

**GOWER HOLIDAY VILLAGE**, Scurlage, Nr Port Eynon, Swansea, S Gower SA3 1AY. Tastefully set in spacious grounds, comfortable two bedroomed bungalows. Facilities include free heated indoor swimming pool, sauna, solarium, games room, putting green, playground, launderette and shop. Tel: 01792 390431. See page 40.

**GREEN LANTERNS GUEST HOUSE**, Hawdref Ganol Farm, Cimla, Neath SA12 9SL. Family run guest house set in 45 acres on hillside. Panoramic views over the Vale of Neath. Tel: 01639 631884. See page 50.

**THE HEYOKAH CENTRE**, 2 Humphrey Street, Swansea SA1 6BG. The Heyokah Centre Vegetarian Restaurant offers elegant dining in natural surroundings. Wholefood cuisine prepared with local organic produce. Open Monday to Saturday, 11.00am – 5.30pm, and evening bookings Thursday, Friday, Saturday from 6.00pm. Tel: 01792 457880. See page 29.

**HILTON NATIONAL SWANSEA**, Phoenix Way, Enterprise Park, Swansea SA7 9EG. The hotel has 118 bedrooms all en suite with TV, telephone and tea/coffee making facilities. Swimming pool, gymnasium, sauna and sunbed. Bar and Restaurant. Tel: 01792 310330. Fax: 01792 797535. See page 19.

**KING ARTHUR HOTEL**, Reynoldston, Gower, Swansea. All bedrooms en suite. B&B from £25 single, £45 double. Extensive bar and restaurant menu. Real ales. Activity holidays catered for by arrangement. Tel: 01792 391099 or 01792 390775. See page 40.

**LA BRASERIA**, 28 Wind Street, Swansea. Good Food • Good Wine. A restaurant with the difference ~ the warm ambience & informality of an authentic Spanish Bodega. Tel: 01792 469683. See page 27.

**NEWPARK HOLIDAY PARK**, Port Eynon, Gower. Newpark lies at the edge of Port Eynon village and has full facilities for touring caravans, trailer tents and tents. Shop, off license, play area, launderette, toilets and showers. Also self catering bungalows. Tel: 01792 390292 / 390478. Fax: 01792 391245. See inside front cover.

## Accommodation & Eating Out

**NICHOLASTON HOUSE HOTEL,** Nicholaston, Gower. Country house hotel set in it's own beautiful grounds. All 13 rooms en suite, colour TV, tea/coffee facilities. A la carte restaurant, weddings/parties, up to 120 catered for. Full size snooker table. Residents lounge. Tel: 01792 371317. See page 41.

**THE NORTH GOWER HOTEL,** Llanrhidian, Gower, Swansea. 16 en suite bedroom hotel set in own grounds overlooking the Loughor Estuary. Bar meals and a la carte restaurant. Tel: 01792 390042. See page 40.

**NO SIGN BAR LTD,** 56 Wind Street, Swansea SA1 1EG. Incorporating the Camelot Function Suite. Salubrious Passage. Kenneth and Elaine Thorpe's Panache Restaurant. Tel: 01792 655332 / 652322. See page 20.

**NUMBER ONE WIND STREET,** 1 Wind Street, Swansea SA1 1DE. Specialising in French Provincial Cuisine and Local Fish & Seafood. Egon Ronay and Good Food Guide Recommended. Tel: 01792 456996. See page 20.

**OAKTREE PARC HOTEL & RESTAURANT LTD,** Birchgrove Road, Birchgrove, Swansea SA7 9JR. Tastefully refurbished gentlemen's country residence, offering all the amenities and comforts of a first class hotel. Superb A La Carte restaurant. Tel: 01792 817781. Fax: 01792 814542. See page 50.

**OXWICH BAY HOTEL,** Oxwich Bay, Gower, Nr Swansea SA3 1LS. Bargain Breaks. Colour brochure on request. Tel: 01792 390329. See page 40.

**OLD WHITE HORSE INN,** High Street, Pontneddfechan, Nr Glynneath. Lunches and evening meals served daily, Tea rooms. Self catering accommodation available. Tel: 01639 721219. See page 54.

**P.A.'S WINE BAR,** 95 Newton Road, Mumbles, Swansea. P.A.'s offers excellent a la carte cuisine cooked to perfection by our expert chefs. Quality wines from around the World. Tel: 01792 367723. See page 33.

**PATRICKS,** 638 Mumbles Road, Southend, Mumbles. Family run business serving seriously good food and drink from Morning Coffee, Lunch Time Specials, Afternoon Tea, Dinner, through to Sunday Lunch. To book a table just contact us on Tel: 01792 360199. See page 34.

**PITTON CROSS CARAVAN AND CAMPING PARK,** Rhossili, Gower. Level site in several small paddocks, near to surfing beaches, coastal path and Worm's Head. Kiddies corner with small animals. Colour brochure a pleasure. Tel: 01792 390593. See page 42.

**PLOUGH & HARROW,** Oldway Road, Murton, South Gower. One of the best known Inns in the area. The Plough & Harrow provides a warm welcome, fine ales and a country fayre menu. Tel: 01792 234459. See page 42.

**THE PLOUGH INN AT RHOSMAEN,** Llandeilo, Carmarthenshire SA19 6NP. Restaurant & bar meals, afternoon teas. En suite accommodation. Highly Commended 4 Crown. Conference facilities. Gym & sauna. Tel: 01558 823431. See page 68.

**SEASONS BISTRO,** 5 & 6 Swan Court, off Gower Road, Killay, Swansea. Incorporating The Village Inn. Freshly prepared continental and traditional cuisine, using locally grown produce. Good selection of wines. Open Tuesday to Saturday. Call for reservations. Tel: 01792 203311. See page 42.

**SHORELINE LEISURE HOME PARK,** Burry Port, Nr Llanelli. Fully equipped, 6-8 berth chalets and caravans for hire or sale. Tourers welcome. Shop, launderette, arcade. Family Club with bar serving Bar Meals and Real Ale. Regular children's entertainment. Tel: 01554 832657. See page 13.

**THE STRADEY PARK,** Furnace, Llanelli. Splendidly situated overlooking Llanelli towards Carmarthen Bay. Open throughout the year. All bedrooms are en suite, with colour TV, tea/coffee making facilities and telephone. Tel: 01554 758171. Fax: 01554 777974. See page 11.

**TREE TOPS GUEST HOUSE,** 282 Neath Road, Briton Ferry, Neath SA11 2SL. Tree Tops offers a warm welcome and good home cooking. Rooms are tastefully furnished. Tel: 01639 812419. See page 50.

**TREASURE,** 29 – 33 Newton Road, Mumbles. Within this gift stor, you will find our Self Serve Restaurant, famous for its "home cooked' foods. Join us for Morning Coffee, Lunch Time Bites or Afternoon Teas. Tel: 01792 361345. See page 33.

**TY'N-Y-CAEAU,** Margam Village, Port Talbot SA13 2NW. 17th Century vicarage in walled gardens. Large en suite bedrooms with mountain and garden views. Close to Margam Abbey and park, and other attractions. Tel: 01639 883897. See page 50.

**WEST CROSS INN & RESTAURANT,** 43 Mumbles Road, West Cross, Swansea. Non-smoking Restaurant open every evening. Bar Lunches. Live music every Thursday. Private Function Room for hire. Large safe Family Garden leading directly onto Promenade and foreshore. Tel: 01792 401143. See page 33.

# Index

**A**
Aberavon 8, 55
Aberdulais Falls 49, 51
Afan Argoed Country Park 56, 59
Afan Lido 8, 55
Afan Valley 55, 56, 59

**B**
Bacon Hole 42
Barry 61
Bishopston 5
Bishop's Wood Nature Reserve 45
Bluepool Bay 6
Bracelet Bay 5, 43
Brandy Cove 5
Bridgend 62
Broughton Bay 6, 8, 41
Broughton Burrows 8
Bryngarw Country Park 62
Burry Holms 6, 41
Burry Port 13

**C**
Candleston Castle 62
Carmarthenshire 67-68
Caswell Bay 5, 43, 45
Cefn Bryn 41
Cefn Sidan Sands 4, 9
Coity Castle 62
Coney Beach Pleasure Park 8, 60, 61, 62
Craig Gwladus Country Park 54
Crawley 6
Culver Hole 42

**D**
Dan-Yr-Ogof Showcaves 54
Dunraven Bay 62

**E**
Eaglebush Valley 54
Eglwys Nunydd Reservoir 59
Ewenny Pottery 62
Ewenny Priory 62

**F**
Fall Bay 6

**G**
Glamorgan Heritage Coast 8, 60, 62
Glamorgan Nature Centre 62
Gnoll Country Park 52
Golf courses & clubs 64
Gower Peninsula 38-46
Great Tor 43

**H**
Horton 6

**K**
Kenfig Burrows 62
Kenfig Nature Reserve 59
Kenfig Sands 8
Kidwelly 10, 15
Kidwelly Castle 9, 15

**L**
Langland 5, 43
Leisure Centres 66
Limeslade Bay 5, 43
Llanelli 4, 9-11
Llangennith 6, 8
Llanmadoc 8
Llanrhidian 46
Llanrhidian Marsh 41, 46
Loughor estuary 8, 9, 41, 46

**M**
Maesteg 62
Margam Abbey 56, 59
Margam Burrows 8
Margam Castle 59
Margam Country Park 8, 55, 56, 59
Margam Sands 8, 55
Melincourt Falls 51
Merthyr Mawr 8, 62
Mewslade Bay 6, 43
Minchin Hole 42
Mumbles 5, 32, 34

**N**
Neath 49, 51-53
Neath Abbey 52
Newcastle Castle 62
Nicholaston Cross 6

**O**
Ogmore-by-Sea 8, 61, 62
Ogmore Castle 46
Ogwr 60-62
Oxwich Bay 6, 43
Oxwich Castle 46
Oystermouth Castle 34

**P**
Parkmill 5, 6
Paviland 42
Pebbles Bay 5
Pennard Castle 6, 43
Pembrey 4, 13
Pembrey Circuit & Motorsports Centre 9, 15
Pembrey Country Park 4, 9, 13, 15
Penclawdd 41
Penclacwydd Wildfowl & Wetland Centre 9, 11
Penmaen 5
Penscynor Wildlife Park 53
Port Eynon 6, 42, 43, 44, 46

Porthcawl 8, 60-62
Port Talbot 8, 55, 56, 59, 61
Pwll Du Bay 5
Pwll Du Head 42

**R**
Rest Bay 8, 61
Rhondda Valley 56
Rhossili 6, 41, 42, 44
Rhossili Down 41
Rotherslade 5, 43

**S**
Sandy Bay 8, 61
Seaside Awards 4
Southerndown 8, 60
Southgate 5, 6
sports & leisure facilities 63-66
Swansea 17-37
Swansea Bay 5, 17-37
swimming pools 66

**T**
Tears Point 43
Thomas, Dylan 17, 20, 27
Three Cliffs Bay 6, 7, 42, 43, 45
Thurba Head 6, 42, 43
Tor Bay 5
Tourist Information Centres 69
Trecco Bay 8, 61

**V**
Vale of Neath 49-54

**W**
Weobley Castle 44, 46
Whiteford Burrows 8, 41
Whiteford Point 8, 41
Whiteford Sands 8, 41
Worms Head 6, 42

## ACKNOWLEDGEMENTS

The author's thanks are due to Ian Smith, of Bézier Design; Haven Colourprint; Tonia Kemp and Nigel Doyle, Swansea City Council; Sue Moore, Llanelli Borough Council; Lyn Rees and Pam Creacroft, Neath Port Talbot County Borough Council; Fiona Rees, Ogwr Borough Council; Jo Exell, Glamorgan Wildlife Trust; the Tidy Britain Group; Linda and Miles Cowsill and Pat and Geoff Somner of Lily Publications; and David Lemon and all the advertisers, whose support has made publication of this guide possible.